WHAT WAS THAT ABOUT?

LEN TABICMAN

ISBN: 978-1-950621-00-2 (paperback)

ISBN: 978-1-950621-01-9 (ebook)

Published by LightHouse Global Publishing and PR LLC

http://www.lighthouseglobalinc.com/

CONTENTS

For Susan, my muse.

1. WOULD YOU PLEASE UPDATE MY STAR CHART WITH MY NEW BIORHYTHMS?

I would like, from the onset, to be brutally honest with you. This may not be your variety of book. I say that in an attempt to save you both time and money. These valuable resources could be better applied elsewhere.

I suggest that it would be admirable if an author would tell you in the first chapter what the book you are intending to read isn't. Yes, isn't. Not what the book is or could be. Or what you want it to be.

If you're looking for a quick fix or a magical solution to the difficulties that life brings to you then you are in the wrong place. The first time I became aware of the fact that there were no enchanted quick-fixes was when I was eighteen. I was working in the Bronx as a stock boy in a part-time position and saving money for college.

At the time, I was supervised by a forty year old man who lived his life according to a series of charts that showed his biorhythms. These charts showed the physical, emotional and intellectual cycles in his life. He

reviewed his charts every morning. If he saw that two of
the cycles crossed, he would have a bad day in those two
areas. Every few months, all three cycles crossed necessi-
tating a day or two off from work to cower in bed, awaiting
a fate which never truly materialized. My simple and
somewhat obvious question is: Were the charts a reflec-
tion of what was happening in his life? Or was he living as
the charts told him to live? I strongly suspect the latter. He
had turned over the control of his life to daily chart read-
ings and modified his behavior to be in accord with the
chart results. He had programmed himself as if he were a
computer, devoid of emotions or choices. Didn't work.
Never even had a chance.

There are so many nonsensical self-help theories and
guides published in a ten billion dollar industry. Studies
show that individuals who purchase self-help books
normally purchase them every 18 months. What's wrong
with this? What in God's name is everyone looking for
and not finding?

To be more definitive, let me tell you what else this
book isn't. As you read, I will not attempt to align or
realign your Chakras. No Chakras here. Many people
have enough difficulty balancing their checkbooks. The
daunting task of balancing your Chakras would be way
above both our pay grades. Furthermore, we will not talk
of Freud, Jung, Erikson or a veritable plethora of other
therapists. I believe they have no real bearing on your
current life situation. No penis envy. No id,. No regression.
No Gestalt. Not here. To add to the list, I propose the
absence of palm reading, tea leaf reading and horoscope
reading.

Let me list some of the other dubious, at least to me, self- help concepts or guides that will not be discussed. Phrenology, horoscopes, card reading, numerology, spirit guides, psychic healers, fortune tellers, the 7 Gates to Freedom, and how stones and rocks are attracted to you. All the teachings of Paramhonsa Yogananda will be absent as will reading crystals and my personal all-time favorite "psychic intuitive and trance channeling" while wearing a pyrite necklace.

After spewing all this negativity, I can freely admit to the fact that there are many useful self-help books such as the 7 Habits books and books by Dale Carnegie. Unfortunately, books such as these are relatively rare and not as cute and trendy as sitting with a spirit guide, wearing moonstone jewelry in the Himalayas, and sipping herbal tea while sweating through a session of hot yoga. You should now have some idea as to what this book isn't. The next logical question is what this book is. Pause, take a moment and clear your mind for a different approach to life's difficulties.

2. HONESTY... IF YOU CAN TAKE IT

I have been a practicing psychotherapist for a little more than forty two years. Over the years, I have heard stories that have amazed me and, at times, there were life narratives that truly bewildered me. I cannot imagine anything, at this point in time, that could astonish me and leave me aghast. I am sure that there are some tales out there that are truly horrific and best avoided by me.

The thinking behind this book is to present numerous case studies and examples of behaviors that shouldn't be modeled in an attempt to learn and profit from the mistakes of others. The hope is that by seeing these blunders, you can look at your own life and make some modifications that will change your future. Yes, you absolutely can learn from the mistakes of others. You will find many people in this book that you see every day in your own life.

Before I continue, there is a question that has been asked of me dozens of times in the past few months. The question is always a variation of the following, "Oh my God! Will I be in your book?" My answer is an absolute, definite, unequivocal "Yes." Of course you will be in the book. Although with some caveats. I will change your name, sex (not literally), age, location, etc. You will be the only person who might be able to identify yourself. So, rest assured, if I know you then there is a distinct possibility that something you have said will be in the following pages.

While we're clearing the air, let me answer a second question that has been repeatedly asked of me. This question is normally asked in social situations where people initially do not know my occupation. I find it truly astonishing to see how all conversation comes to a total standstill when people find that they are talking to a psychotherapist. Animate, lively conversation full of laughter and joy stops as if Jimmy Hoffa had just walked into the room. The question is always basically the same. People want to know if I've been analyzing them and the things they've said. I always respond to this query by saying that I turn the meter off the second I leave my office at the end of the day. Unfortunately, this is a falsehood. An untruth. A barefaced lie.

In actuality, there never has been a meter as years of training have conditioned me to question why people say and do the things they do. Always in a loving manner of course. Consider this simple example. Recently, I stopped off at a new neighbor to drop off some paperwork related to our home association. She was working in her flower garden in front of her house. I told her that her garden was beautiful and that it must require a great deal of hard work. She launched into a description of her 5 bedroom, 5,000 square foot house in northern New Jersey on 1.6 acres with over fifty varieties of shrubs and flowers that needed constant care. She told me that it costs her in excess of four thousand dollars a year to maintain her arboretum because "good help is so hard to find." Most people would have been impressed and simply moved on. My question was why did she have a need to tell me her acreage, the number of bedrooms, the size of her house in response to my one simple statement?

That's just the way my mind works, at times utterly out of my own control. I can't help thinking why people say the things they say. For me, it's an automatic response that does not require any additional effort. It just happens, like riding a bike or salivating over a good pastrami sandwich.

This book is based upon truth and honesty. The first step in dealing with any complex situation is to evaluate the problem realistically and objectively. This presupposes an ability to be able to assess oneself and to deal with self-reflection in a straight forward mature fashion. This is a very difficult task that requires constant reexamination and the need to accept feedback from others.

In my final year in college, two of my friends were planning to get married in June. We will call her Liz and call him Bob. Starting in January or February of that year, Liz would ask me, at least two or three times a week, if I felt that she should lose weight. Since I had fully functioning neurons, I avoided giving her an answer. I told her that she should ask Bob. Despite all of her attempts over the ensuing months, I was able to avoid falling into the obvious trap. Wedding invitations were mailed and I was honored to be chosen to be an usher at their wedding. Liz never stopped with her questions. One day, in early May, she came to me in tears asking for my honesty and an answer. Thinking back, I must have been influenced by bad cafeteria food in combination with the light glinting off of Liz's tears because I entered a realm totally foreign to most men. Maybe it was a short term thinking seizure. Or a thought convulsion. Or even possibly an immense brain fart that totally overtook my rationality. You know where I'm going with this. I told her that if weight was such a concern, she ought to "consider taking off a few pounds." Notice I said a few pounds and nothing more. "Get rid of one of those chins" or get a badly needed belly roll reduction" was called for, but I graciously said only a few pounds. From that day until today, a period of fifty years, Liz has not spoken one word to me. This silent treatment included muteness at the wedding and all subsequent parties with our mutual group of friends. Not one single solitary word. Not a wave, a smile, nor a grunt. I surmised that honesty and feedback just was not her thing but it was a good thing for me. It was a great learning experience.

Two final topics need to be discussed before moving on: accurate reality and doing "the work." Reality is the state of being real, factual, truthful and authentic. You can't change reality despite monumental efforts. Many difficulties are compounded by a simple inability to accept what is staring you in the face. In college I had a friend who lost a finger in a childhood accident. Everything that happened to him from that fateful digit losing day was in some way connected to his finger. Girls didn't

like him because he had only nine digits. College professors didn't like him and would lower his grades as they
were offended by his malady. Cat's would hiss at his finger
as he walked by them and dogs would howl. Life was just
so unfair to have burdened him with such a terrible affliction. It's just a finger for God's sake. Not the end of the
Universe. But, he chose to make this the focal point of his
existence and refused to accept the reality of the missing
finger. Reality does, in fact, bite at times and you may not
like it. However, it remains a factual, truthful, authentic
and unmodifiable entity.

Now, a few words on doing the work involved in therapy. If a patient attends therapy once a week for fifty
minutes then goes home and continues to do what he or
she has always done then therapy will without doubt fail.
Change takes a good deal of work and fifty minutes a
week won't cut it. Even with a fabulous therapist and the
best intentions. Change should be noticeable by both the
therapist and the patient over time. I have a therapist
friend who constantly brags about two clients who have
been coming to see him for over ten years. The only thing
that has changed is an increase in my friend's bank
account with a corresponding decrease in his patient's
retirement accounts.

He's really not such a terrific friend, but more about
him in future chapters. As you continue to read, you
should think about what you can realistically change and
what you can't. You should formulate a plan with goals
that are modifiable to account for any ailment that may
step in your way. Such as the loss of a finger.

Now, I will administer a short non-graded test to see if

you are really paying attention. This past weekend, my wife and I attended a music and food festival in a small town near where we live. We were sitting on a bench, listening to music and minding our own business. Out of the blue, an overdressed, bejeweled couple sat down next to us. Unexpectedly, the man said that the weather was going to get bad. Note that I did not ask him about the weather. I nodded and told him that the sky looked clear. So far everything is evolving but we had no idea where he was going with the conversation. Very quickly, it became abundantly clear when he said, "I have a classic, fully restored, red 1965 Mustang convertible that we drove here today for the car show. But, it might rain. Every time, we bring one of our classic cars to a show this kind of stuff happens. Gotta run now! See you guys."

Ask yourself: What was that all about? What was his motivation? What did he hope to accomplish? Why all the details unrelated to anything? About an hour after our short conversation with Mr. Mustang, it did start to rain cats and dogs. For some sick inexplicable reason, I enjoyed the hell out of that rain.

3. THIS IS ME - A VERY SHORT AUTO BIOGRAPHY

On September 1, 1975, without the slightest degree of trepidation, I proudly opened my office in Teaneck, New Jersey to practice the art of psychotherapy. In retrospect, if I had known then what I learned over the next forty two years, three months and six days, I would have begun with somewhat less confidence and a tad more apprehension.

I was totally confident that I would be able to treat any and all mental disorders ranging from mild mood disorders to full blown schizophrenia. After extensive coursework, an externship and an internship, I was, as they say, ready to go. I feel differently now, kind of like the insurance ad on television that says "We know a thing or two because we've seen a thing or two." I've seen and heard more than a thing or two and can only marvel at my lack of expertise during my early years as a psychotherapist.

My auspicious practice began with two patients. Both female and both in their 30s. Clara was a total delight. She was what I really needed at that time to prove to myself that I could actually be a competent therapist. She was bright and enthusiastic with a burning desire to deal with her problems in a straightforward proactive manner. Clara had some significant relationship difficulties with her mother and younger sister. Therapy progressed like clockwork. She gained insight and became more aware of her unique difficulties. She developed a toolbox full of approaches to deal with her problems. She decided to change and success was on the horizon.

Kim was another case altogether. Initially a little shy and withdrawn, she warmed up slowly during the first few sessions until she was comfortable in the therapeutic setting. She stated that her difficulty was work related as she was not getting along with many people in her office. What I was to find out later, after years of practice, was that the presenting problem was often not the real problem. Kim was attractive, verbal and obviously extremely bright (she reported an IQ. of 138). She was always very well dressed, wearing layers of brightly coordinated outfits all in the fashion of the day.

In mid-September of that year, after seeing Kim for a few weeks, we had a succession of hot and humid days. On one of these days, Kim again presented in her stylish coordinated layers. But why was she wearing at least three layers of clothing in the hot and humid weather? The reality was that at a height of 5 feet 6 inches, Kim admitted to a weight of 90 pounds. I suspected that she weighed considerably less than that. So there I was with one animated and exhilarated patient and a second client with a significant eating disorder.

I wasn't comfortable with treating Kim's disorder so I

did what any competent therapist would do, I researched. I studied anorexia, bulimia, body dysmorphic disorders and a slew of lesser disorders. I studied the origins, the causes, the treatments, the medications and the prognosis. I was as ready as I could be to effectively work with Kim. Or so I thought. Even with all of my training and hours of research, I was woefully unprepared to work with her. It was totally my problem, not hers. There was something about me that brought my level of discomfort to newfangled highs. The question now was to determine what it was about me that brought out this uneasiness. I realized that, in order, to be an effective therapist, I would need to know myself better. Much better.

What I found out over the next few months is something I had known intuitively about myself for years. However, I was unaware of the effect it had on me. I recognized the fact that I was a logical, sequential thinker. If there is a simple and logical solution to a problem then the problem should be easily solved. Anorexia is a slow, tortuous, self-imposed death. In my simplistic view, it was difficult to conceive of an individual starving oneself to death while there was an abundance of food available. I wanted to stop off on the way to the office and get Kim two Whoppers, large fries and a shake. I could just sit and watch her eat and the problem would be taken care of. I knew then as I know now that there are an incredible number of factors that results in anorexia. But, why not just eat while we figure it all out? Try to picture yourself not eating over an extended period until you are so weak that you expire? This was impossible for me to envision. If there was a simple remedy at hand, why would you not jump at it? Depressed individuals have no difficulty taking anti-depressants. People in pain take pain relievers and food is available for anorexics. I'm not professing to be right about my views. In fact, I know that I'm way off the mark with regard to eating disorders but that's a great thing to know about yourself if you're a therapist.

After taking a good look at myself, I decided that it would be in everyone's best interest if I would not treat eating syndromes. I saw Kim for a few exasperating sessions before referring her to an overweight psychiatrist friend of mine who specialized in eating complaints. His office was only four or five blocks from mine, next to a McDonald's and a Burger King. Interesting.

I was brought up in a middle class home with a number of rules. One of the rules was that you always clean your plate because there were millions of children starving in Europe. This must have been working in my subconscious for years, thinking about children my age without enough food to survive. Even as an adult, if I was at a buffet and I saw someone with a heaping mound of food, I wanted to go to that person and tell him or her that they'd better eat everything on their plate. I am no longer permitted to eat at Sally's All You Can Eat Buffet. Nor am I permitted to go near the Wendy's salad bar. I guess I was kind of annoying some customers. But, I still think I was right. As a therapist, you have an obligation to your patients and yourself to understand your areas of strength and, even more importantly, your weaknesses.

I would like to tell you a little something else to better explain how my personality was molded. I was born in Bronx, New York. I have an older brother and a younger sister. Both of my parents were what we would call white collar workers and it seemed that we had the same tangibles as everyone else in our neighborhood. Nothing ostentatious. No new cars. No travels to Europe and definitely no bling jewelry. My brother still says that I was the pampered middle child although I recall my childhood quite differently. What I do know is that I developed a relatively quick wit and a remarkable appreciation for humor. Elementary school and high school were relatively uneventful. I came into my own in undergraduate school. As the first college student in the family, I was so impressed with myself that I became a tad annoying.

During my freshman year, I came across a book called "On Human Symbiosis and the Vicissitudes of Individuation." I immediately went to the college bookstore and purchased the only copy that had been on the shelf for nine years. So far, nothing wrong. However, the next step took me on a giant leap to the world of obnoxious. I carried that book with me everywhere, to school, on the train, to movies, to the deli and to bed. During all these times, I would make sure that the spine, with the title, was facing out so that everyone could infer how brilliant I was. I now look at middle-aged people who wear Harley Davidson leather jackets, Mercedes sweaters or Yacht Club t-shirts in the same light as my carrying my book. What are they really saying? They're saying, "Please look at me! I'm terrific and rich and wonderful." I was over my stint of obnoxiousness at twenty one but many of my acquaintances in their fifties, sixties, and seventies are still doing the same thing on a daily basis.

Within a week of discovering my most cherished book,

I came upon a disorder named phenylpyruvic oligophrenia. Captivated by this impressive malady, I tried to work
this little ditty into everyday conversations. Not an easy
task. I was twenty years old when I was able to vocalize
this tongue twister. My brother, who was three years older
and somewhat shorter had just walked in from work after
a very draining day. I said, "Are you okay? Because you
look like you could have a slight case of phenylpyruvic
oligophrenia." He looked at me for a full minute and then
beat me up. Not a bad beating but one that I will
remember forever for the words he said after the beating
were the true punishment. He looked me in the eye and
softly said, "You're an idiot." Unfortunately, in retrospect, I
see that he was right. My need to impress was squashed
on that day.

Wouldn't it be wonderful if everyone knew themselves? The good, the bad, and, particularly the ugly?
Knowing your strengths and becoming aware of your
weaknesses is a sure and definite path to good mental
health... and happiness.

4. PERSONAL LEARNING EXPERIENCES

E veryone has the capacity to learn and everyone learns differently and at a different rate. Sometimes, what we learn is quickly forgotten. Other times, our unique learning experiences can last a lifetime. At times, these experiences are determining factors. They shape our personalities. But, most times, these occurrences are very trivial and mostly forgotten. Here are a few of my own encounters with learning that illustrate that if the small occurrences can have meaning, then the major learning episodes should never be ignored.

Attending school in the third grade in New York, there was a memorable student named Heinz in my class. He was not bright and he was not, in any sense, attractive. However, he was massive. He was huge, immense and stupendously gigantic from the top of his swollen head to his clenched fists that looked like swollen lobster claws. On a cold winter day, I was doing my best impression of Heinz to the delight of my friends. Unbeknown to me, at some point, he came up from behind and listened, very quietly, to my riotous comic performance. I found out very quickly that Heinz had, despite all of his other attributes, no sense of humor. For the remainder of the third grade year and the beginning of the fourth, he punished me. I experienced ongoing pain at every level from his infamous headlock to his gently kneading of my youthful ribs with his ham hocks. Thank God he moved in the fourth grade. Possibly to join the Marines. Or to work in the construction field.

A simple lesson is to be careful what you say about people as it may come back to haunt you for years to come. To this day, I get nauseous if someone puts Heinz ketchup in front of me.

When Heinz left, I had a new sense of freedom and the return of sensation to many parts of my body. The second lesson that I took away from these experiences is that making people laugh was something I was very good at. I found, over the years, that humor can diffuse a very uncomfortable situation. It also worked as a coping mechanism for my own anxiety. People actually like to laugh. Just about everyone likes a good chortle and guffaw with the possible exception of Richard Nixon. Knowing when to be funny and when to shut up is also a skill that developed. I needed to use my censors on a regular basis to stop my mouth from getting me into a great deal of trouble. A strange thing about humor is that it's virtually impossible to learn and develop. It's akin to the terrible dancer that you see flailing away on the dance floor. Ten years of Arthur Murray will give him robot like movements. But, will he move like a true dancer? Highly unlikely.

My third lesson involved my mother and her need to

yell at me and my siblings at a decibel level similar to a jet engine at fifteen feet. Don't get me wrong, I love the heck out of my mom. Yelling was her main thing and we all adjusted to it. Except for the cat who ran to her litter box every time the yelling began.

One day, when I was about ten, my brother and I were caught throwing wadded clumps of toilet paper down on people from our fourth floor window. Unfortunately, one of our love bouquets landed on Mr. Grisham, the building tyrant. He had a heated discussion with my mother. After their chat, Mom sat us down and started talking to us. Notice I said talking in a normal tone of voice. Not yelling. For fifteen minutes, and for the first time ever, we saw what Mom was like when she was really, truly angry. Her quiet controlled speech forecast dire consequences. I learned that it is virtually impossible to tell what is going on with some individuals from their outward appearance. This is a significant and critical skill to master if you are to be successful as a therapist.

The final learning experience that provided me with insight regarding my lack of coordination has been useful to me since junior high school. I attended a school in the Bronx named Public School 80. Why a number and not a name was a question that we never pondered. I must admit coming up with a meaningful school ditty was painful at best and although we were in better melodic shape than the poor kids in P.S. 149.

It was at P.S 80 where I took a musical aptitude test. In the spring of 1957, all eighth grade students were brought to Mrs. Micals' music class and given a sheet of paper numbered from one to fifty. Mrs. Micals, adorned with her pearls, horn rimmed glasses and blue hair, cautioned us to take the exercise very, very seriously. Sitting erect at her piano, she played one note followed quickly by a second note. We were to determine if the second note was higher or lower than the first note. Some of the notes were so dissimilar that I began to wonder if this was actually a test for frustration tolerance as I was very close to screaming by number fifty. I couldn't imagine getting even one incorrect. Everyone in the class, except possibly George Hendrick was sure to get 100%. Unfortunately, George had a habit of eating his pencils and he was subsequently unleaded by question twenty-six. Feeling proud of myself, after the test I found out from George of all people what the test was about. It seemed that everyone else knew the real purpose but, for some reason, I never got the memo or the smoke signal.

The musical aptitude test was used to determine what instrument would be assigned to us the next year in the ninth grade. I was hoping for the drums, or if that was not available the infamous triangle, or a bell or a tuning fork. I envisioned myself aptly playing suites, rondos, nocturnes and concertos on my instrument. My instrument and I would fuse into one mellifluous entity like B.B. King or Eric Clapton.

On the first day of school in the ninth grade, we were given our aptitude grade and, sure enough, I nailed it: 100%. That same afternoon, we all lined up to receive our assigned instruments and I was given a leather case approximately eighteen inches long by fourteen inches wide. I opened it up and saw that it was a clarinet. What?! There were so many dials and it looked so confusing. I would have to blow at one end and, at the same time, use my fingers independently to bring further musical sounds. As they say, there lies the problem.

Most people have neurons that work in a coordinated fashion to produce intricate finger movements. The brain functions as the king and sends the fingers messages to tell them what to do. Not so with me as there appears to be a total disconnect between my brain, my neurons and my fingers. I think I may possibly have an inborn genetic defect stemming from an ancestor misusing an ax or something like that. Nevertheless, I was left with a lifelong crippling musical disability.

I grandly plowed through the year, sending my cat back to the litter box every time I would practice. Animals would be drawn to the discordant sounds and, one day, I counted a record eleven squirrels outside of my window. I knew I was bad, but I never knew just how bad I was until, towards the end of my ninth grade year, my neighbors made a simple request. They asked my parents to stop giving me clarinet lessons and for me to start a new career as a listener. Truth be told, I was elated out of my mind and truly thankful for my neighbor's honesty and pluck. This was a significant learning point for me and the knowledge that I have a neural disconnect has saved me from a number of situations that could have ranged from uncomfortable to disastrous. This is how we learn. This is what makes our experiences and our lives. This is what many people are unable to do.

5. AFTER COMMITTING AN UNSPEAKABLE ACT, HE BEGAN MAKING CHICKEN SOUNDS

Nearing the end of my first full year of private practice, Christine came to me for help with some family matters. Christine, who preferred to be called Chris, was a 46 year old, white female, impeccably dressed in a business suit accompanied with a leather briefcase and a matching umbrella. What was most striking about her appearance was her flawless natural gray hair color and the total absence of makeup. Reticent for only the first few minutes, she was remarkably verbal and intelligent once she began to speak. She had been working for the same Fortune 500 corporation for twenty-one years and held a relatively high level position. She was somewhat high strung and agitated. She constantly clutched a very large gold cross worn on an oversized chain. After obtaining all the basic information, I asked her to tell me how I can be of assistance. This was her response as close to verbatim as I remember:

"I really don't know where to begin. I have so much to tell you so I guess I'll just ramble along and you can tell me where to stop. Let's see, where should I begin? I guess a lot of what I have to tell you will sound insignificant and even downright petty but here goes. I hope you're ready. I have been married to my husband Al for twenty four and a half years and we expect to celebrate our wonderful twenty fifth in just five months. I'm being a bit sarcastic. The last word I would really use is wonderful. So, let's see we'll start with the dog which I adore. Trixie is a rescue dog now eight years old. Al, my husband, has never walked the dog with the exception of the one time I was in the hospital for gall bladder operation. If you do the math, I have walked Trixie twice a day for a little over eight years, a total of almost 6,000 times compared to his once. The only contact he has with Trixie is when he taunts her by pretending to have a treat. He thinks it's hilarious and guffaws when he teases her. I think it's contemptible. In addition, he has fed her only one day during those eight years. Again, due to my hospital stay. I know this must sound somewhat inconsequential but there are so many little things that just keep adding up and have brought me to the point where I stay awake just hating him and hoping that some unexpected misfortune is on the horizon for him. Oh God, I can't believe I just said that.

To continue, Al has never cooked a meal in all these years unless you count opening a can of chili or ravioli as a tasty treat for his own consumption. It's as if he's allergic to the metal in pots and pans. He just can't seem to be able to figure out that tricky oven and those complicated burners. After our meals, he leaves the table and refuses to bring his plates to the sink where I await, like his personal slave, to clean after him. Then, he makes himself comfortable on the couch with a beer and chips and tries to set a new flatulence record for men over fifty. Personally, I believe that he has broken the record for North and South America. Am I sounding mean? I really don't like to talk like this but you need to know it all. So, I'll just keep rolling along.

When he sporadically takes a shower, you can bet that the towels are left on the floor despite many of my own personal infomercials about the wonders of towel bars. Ditto for the soap. Apparently, the soap dish is a bit too far for his chubby little arms to reach so the soap is also left on the floor. Our laundry is done every other day and always by- Guess who? Me. That's right! I have done all the laundry since our wonderful honeymoon in Jamaica, Queens. Not the Jamaica with images of white sand beaches and palm trees. No. Not with Al. We spent a glorious five nights with his brother and his wife in Jamaica, New York watching a succession of baseball games... Whoopee-do! Let me continue. Food shopping and clothes shopping is done by yours truly as Al hates big stores and has an aversion to trying things on so I spend a great deal of time in the local food stores and even more time trying to find shirts for his seventeen inch plump neck. I don't know if I should just keep on with my tirade or if I need to stop. If it's okay, I'll just keep going. I have to admit that it's beginning to feel pretty good to finally unload all of this rubbish.

Weekends at our house consist of him sitting on the couch, watching television and smoking cigarettes and cigars. He is totally unaware of the stench that surrounds both him and his ashtray which is always filled to the

brim. Whenever an ad comes on the television warning of the dangers of smoking, he calls it fake news and hits the mute button. As far as personal hygiene goes, that is a concept that totally escapes his conscious mind. He bathes no more than once a week and gets a haircut approximately every two months whether he needs it or not. Needless to say, he's repulsive to be around unless you're lucky enough to catch him on one of his sporadic spa bath days.

Now, I believe that I'm ready to tell you the really annoying and disturbing things about my paramour. Let's start with his weight. I believe I can diplomatically call him obese. I would imagine that he's about seventy-five to a hundred pounds over where he should be. Doc, do you know how some people have extra weight and they carry it very well? Not so in his case. You could say that he carries his poundage very poorly. Couple this with an unkempt, rough beard and the absence of at least ten or twelve teeth and you have the Marlborough Man of the year. You know, Doc, as I'm telling you all this, I feel a sense of betrayal. At the same time, something about this feels really, really good.

Finally, here are the four things that I cannot live with anymore. Plus one unspeakable act that has my head spinning. Number one is the fact that he has only gone to church with me once since I know him. I am a devout Roman Catholic and I believe that attending church services twice a week is the right thing to do. He doesn't believe in the teachings of any church and I suspect he has no belief in God. I have to attend all of the numerous functions that take place during the year solo. This makes me terribly uncomfortable. My friends repeatedly ask where my husband is and I suspect that they all know that something is not quite right in Shangri-la. The second of the big four is the fact that since I've known Al, he has told me he loved me twice. Yes, two times in more than twenty-five years. I remember them both like they were yesterday. The first time was when he asked me to marry him. I told him that I couldn't marry a man who couldn't say he loved me. To shut me up and to agree to the marriage, he quickly mumbled that he loved me. The second time was in Jamaica, Queens, on the first night of our honeymoon, when I, again, demanded that he say those wonderful words. Once again, he quickly mumbled the words then he mounted me for two minutes, grunted and has never repeated those words to this day. Forget Valentine's Day, birthdays, anniversaries and all the other important dates as they have no meaning for poor, brain-less shithead Al.

Number three of the final four has to do with my family and his hatred for them. Every last one of them. I could list all the family members that he dislikes but it would be easier to simply state that he hates them all equally. This includes my parents, my two sisters, their husbands and their children including a nine month old niece. Also included are grandparents, nephews, great aunts and uncles and anyone with the same last name as ours. He has managed to separate me from my family to the point that he has not attended any family function for more than fifteen years.

Finally, the last of the big four is difficult for me to talk about although I did speak to my priest about this issue.

He told me that it was an appropriate subject to discuss. It has to do with sex. The honeymoon coupling that was short lived and unpleasant was followed a year later with another two minute union that left everything to be desired. If you're waiting for me to tell you about number three or four or five, you'll be waiting as long as I have. That's it. The magic number is two. In twenty five years! When I tried talking to him about sex, he told me that I had a carnal problem and needed help. For years, I truly believed that there was something seriously wrong with me and that the problem was mine. It was only after I talked to the priest that I realized that he has never fulfilled his end of the marriage commitment in the eyes of God. Now, the topic of sex never comes up by either of us. It's a totally dead issue. In the past, whenever I tried to broach the topic he would tell me that he was exhausted from changing tires all day. I've been replaced by Goodyear and Michelin. Where the rubber meets the road. Those are the only rubbers that have ever been in our house. He has been changing tires for the same company for twenty one years. He's still making slightly above minimum wage but with the benefits of filthy nails and repulsive body odor."

She chatted on for another twenty minutes basically repeating much of the same information. I remained totally receptive, unable to get any words in as she had a need to unload. She told me that she enjoyed our session and that she would like to come in once a week to work on "things." The unspeakable act was to be discussed in a week as she needed to meet with the priest again and then go shopping, walk the dog, cook and you already know the rest of her day.

A week later, Chris returned for her session and was once again impeccably attired and coiffed although a little tense. She exuded an air of confidence that I had not seen preciously. She told me that she had a much better week but she really didn't know why she felt so much better. She asked me if she should just blather on as she did last week. I told her to blather to her heart's content.

"I guess you need to know what finally brought me here after all these years. A few weeks ago, I was having lunch with my sister and I can honestly thank her for being my own personal catalyst. She told me that she wanted to plan something very special for my twenty-fifth anniversary in five months. When she said those words something hit me like a bolt of lightning that seared my brain. I remember that I was unable to speak for a few minutes and my sister was concerned that I was stroking out. I recall repeating out loud that I could not be married to that man for twenty five years. I just repeated the same thing over and over while my sister became increasingly concerned. It hit me all at once. The idea of spending all those years with this man was incomprehensible and something that I could not and would not do in my lifetime.

As luck would have it, a few days later, I realized that I could run home for lunch and talk this out with Al. He worked five minutes from our house so he went home to eat and to be intentionally messy with his lunch every day. My intent was to surprise him and catch him off guard so that I could say what I needed to say before he gathered himself and cut me off like he always does. What happened next shocked me so badly that it's still hard for me to believe that it really happened. But, it did.

I opened the door and was surprised at how quiet the house was so I walked into our bedroom and found Al naked from the waist down masturbating. He chose to perform this wonderful act on my dirty clothes that were in the laundry basket in my closet. At first, he wasn't aware of the fact that I was standing there and until he slowly raised his head and let go of his penis which he once laughingly called Thor. He stood without moving a muscle for about 10 seconds which is an extremely long time in an uncomfortable situation like that. Then, he started to make a strange noise, coming from deep in his throat that sounded like a chicken clucking. I could not wrap my head around the idea of my husband masturbating on my dirty clothes and then making chicken sounds when he was caught. I grabbed my purse and ran from the house too confused to process the whole ordeal. I'm sure that the symbolism and the hidden meanings behind his behavior could keep me in therapy for years but I'm choosing to leave it as it is. I may never eat chicken again. I'd like to leave all that alone, at least for now, and get down to what he's done this week."

Finally, my chance to speak, the opening I'd been waiting for. I said "You don't have to tell me anything as I'm pretty sure that I can tell you what has and hasn't happened this past week. Indulge me and let me give it a try. We'll start with the basics and the things he didn't do which probably include walking or feeding the dog, preparing any meals or cleaning up after himself at the end of a meal. I would also imagine that he has bathed only once or twice during the past week and each time he has left his towels on the floor and the soap a mess. During the past week, I would wager that he has not shopped either for food or clothing and that whatever clothing has been worn was washed by you. Furthermore, and not to sound nasty but I'd imagine that he is still grossly overweight and is still missing a significant number of teeth. He probably has not gone to church nor spent time with your family nor had any extensive meaningful conversation with you. What he has definitely done in the short span of seven days is tease the dog, eat chips, drink beer, and set a world's record for flatulence. Two other things that he has not done would include telling you that he loves you and making love to you.

What you have done is to repeat the same cycle daily for almost twenty five years and yet you continue to become enraged with his very predictable behavior. I can tell you right now what your next week will be like and the week after that and so on. What's really going on here?
"

We began to discuss the predictability of his behavior and, more importantly, why she hasn't been able to break the disturbing cycle of activity on both their parts. When all was said and done, Chris was living an unfulfilled life that repeated itself endlessly and would continue until she did something to end the cycle of misery. It seems that her religious background and very strong feelings about marriage had a lot to do with her accepting her current situation. She was worried that God would be unhappy with her if she left her marriage and, furthermore, that she would be punished. Punished in what way she didn't know but the wrath of God would make her life a living hell. What turned Chris around was the fact that if she stayed with Al, she could expect decades of the same life. The thought bordered on intolerable. She also came to realize that God would not single her out for punishment and that, in all likelihood, God would prefer if she were happy. This is an easy concept for many but it was a game changer and a very difficult concept for Chris to accept. In the end, Chris was able to get an annulment from Al with significant help from her priest as it was shown that he had not fulfilled his marital obligations. Two years after the annulment, she met the owner of her favorite Italian restaurant. A year after, she was married to this truly caring and spiritual man. Chicken was not served at the wedding.

Psychology has been loosely defined as the study of behavior. At one point, it was defined as the study of the mind. No one was able to clearly define exactly what the "mind" was. The true value of psychology is to be able to predict future behavior by investigating present and past behaviors. In Chris' case, prediction was relatively easy as her patterns were very clear. Most times, you have to dig for quite some time to discern clear patterns. Too much emphasis is spent trying to predict behavior after the fact as opposed to looking towards the future. Whenever there is a killing or multiple murders, the first thing we want to know is what were the signs and why couldn't we stop that person from taking five guns to a school and killing twenty defenseless people.

So, what is the lesson to be learned from Chris? Take

the time to look at your life. Look into your magic mirror and see your life in a year or three years or ten years. The difficult step is realistically evaluate where you're heading and decide to make some meaningful changes to point you in a more positive direction and actually change your life.

6. AM I CRAZY?

One of the questions my patients have asked repeatedly over the years is a variation of "Am I crazy?", "Am I nuts?" or "Is there something seriously wrong with me?" and so on. Before you can consider the concept of "crazy," you have to be able to get a handle on what is "normal." To quote directly from Webster, normal is "conforming with or constituting an accepted standard, model, or pattern corresponding to the median or average of a large group." In other words, does your behavior fit in with what is generally considered acceptable? To truly complicate matters, you have to take into account the specific circumstances where the behavior occurs. For example, if you are in a restaurant and you begin to scream and yell profanities while jumping up in the air then you will quickly be removed from the premises. However, if you are in a stadium in Liverpool, watching a soccer match and your team scores, you'd better be jumping, screaming and cursing.

Culturally normal is even more complicated as it refers to the culture in general and all the subcultures we live in. If all twenty four of your friends now have piercings in various body parts and you have none then you are out of the average for that group. If you then pierce your eyelids and your nose, you need to stay away from Mom's church group for quite some time as you do not fit their custom. If you hang with the jocks and you have an A average in school, you may be out of their average. If you wear a very low cut dress to your third grader's talent show, you would definitely be out of the standard. In a general sense, if you fit into the group or the culturally accepted behavior, you are in the norm or standard.

It becomes more and more complex as the term "normal" is dependent on numerous other factors. What most people can agree on is the concept of statistically normal. For example, if the normal height for a thirty year old man is 5'10' and you are 4'6' then you are in the abnormal (horrible word) range. Same applies for someone 6'10' while possibly a great basketball center he or she is outside of the typical. Same applies to weight, hair color (a ginger in Sweden) body shape (anorexia), body size (morbidly obese), intellect (either a genius or very low functioning) and numerous other factors.

So, if we have such a hard time defining normal, how can we possibly define "crazy?" As it happens "crazy" is a lot easier to define than you'd think. Once again quoting from Webster, "crazy" is "unsound of mind; mentally unbalanced or deranged, psychopathic, insane." This definition is only marginally helpful because it only gives you a sense of the concept of "crazy." My own definition is that any behavior taken to excess that interferes with normal life functioning would be considered abnormal. In addition, the behaviors must, in some way, impact the individual and cause some form of psychological imbalance. Let us imagine a woman who washes her hands thirty times a day. Sounds like excessive hand washing until you find out that she works in a dental office. That same number of thirty for a housewife staying at home is way out of line. Take any behavior to excess and you begin to see where people cross the line into the dimension of the deviant.

What is the norm for sexual intercourse for a couple married for five years? While five times a week might be okay for one couple, another duo may be very happy with once a week. At the either extremes of the continuum, some people have sex twice a day and other people have sex once a year or every decade. The same concept of abnormal applies to almost every behavior known to man (or woman). What constitutes abnormal eating? Eating way too much or way too little would be abnormal. What is normal for the following: washing your car, cleaning your house, washing your windows, the number of showers you take each day, how much you talk, how little you talk, how much you read, how much time you spend on the computer, how much you cry, how much you laugh and so on. Fortunately for all of us, the word "crazy" is not a word used by professionals as it is impossible to define. At one point in time, there was a clear distinction between levels of abnormality. The simplified breakdown was normal, neurotic, and psychotic. A long standing example to show the differences between the three designations is to look at people buying lottery tickets. The normal individual will occasionally buy a ticket and spend some brief time thinking about what to do with the windfall. The neurotic spends a great deal of time ruminating over what yacht to buy, what house to purchase and what a five carat ring would cost. The psychotic, prior to finding out if his or her numbers match the winning numbers, would sign the papers for the new yacht, house and ring. Nowadays, the bible for psychologists is a book entitled the DSM-5 with hundreds of pages categorizing all mental illnesses. It includes illnesses ranging from mental retardation to ADHD to PTSD to depression and the better known maladies such as bipolar disorders, depressive disorders, schizophrenia and caffeine intoxication. An example is probably in order.

Julie was a 31 year old professional college student. When I first saw her, she was working on her second doctorate and already had a bachelor's degree, two Master's degrees and a PhD In the field of economics. Aside from a short stint at Burger King when she was nineteen, she had never been gainfully employed. The job at Burger King lasted about ten days as it seems that every employee did everything wrong all the time. Julie presented as a short, slightly overweight woman with extremely long braided hair and what looked to be a very intricate bun on top of her head. She was verbal, bright and engaged very easily during our first session. The first sign of difficulty actually occurred before our first session while trying to set up an appointment. When we discussed my openings for the week, she told me that she could not come in for any appointment if the time was an odd hour such as 1 o'clock, 3 o'clock and so on. We agreed to a 2 o'clock appointment and I assured her that she would be done before the witching hour of 3. In addition, she informed me that she considers Monday to be the first day of the week and since this was the case, she could only see me on even days which she emphatically stated were Tuesday and Thursday. I was intrigued with the prospect of a full blown OCD client as I knew a few things about them that I liked. First of all, they were always on time. Secondly, they always had their checks made out before the session. No cancellations were on the horizon as OCD patients would show up even with a case of Ebola or Zika.

During our sessions, Julie opened up readily while discussing her behavior which she felt was just slightly off. It seems that her alarm clock is always set for her to wake up at even times. Bedtime, as you probably can guess, was always at an even hour and minute. When doing the laundry, she would count how many times she would need to take the clothes from the washer to the dryer. If it was an even number, she was fine. But, if it was an odd number, the clothes went back into the washer to be taken out again. Julie told me that on her bad days she might go through this process three or four times. Her highest recorded number was seven which she attributed to doing her laundry on a Monday. Julie further noted that she washed her hands ten to twenty times a day and always washed them twice so that she had an even number of washes. She only read the newspaper on even days and television was an even day experience. Food also proved to be a major obstacle in her life. For example, if she ordered fish or spare ribs, she would become upset if they were an odd number and, at times, would lose her appetite. In addition, she would hose down the street in front of the house every day at either 4 or 6 o'clock. She would only answer the phone on the second, fourth or sixth ring. Her cleaning disorder was totally out of control but two things finally brought her to therapy. The first issue came to light when she had a girlfriend over for drinks and her girlfriend asked for ice. Julie had a need to wash the ice under the faucet much to the surprise of her friend. After an intense ice cube washing her friend told her that she was "strange and a bit peculiar." She took this statement to heart and began to feel the need to get some help. The second sign was an episode in a fast food establishment where she asked the counter clerk to make sure that she was given an even number of French fries or she couldn't accept them. The under-employed, under-paid worker looked at her, and according to Julie told her to go to the nut store where she'd feel more at home. These two incidents occurred within 24 hours of each other and brought Julie to my office not a minute too soon.

The question that remains is a simple one: Is Julie normal? Abnormal? Or even "crazy?" The answer, as usual, is very complex. If Julie remained at home with an occasional visitor, she would appear normal. If Julie ventured out and imposed her OCD on other people she would be regarded as different and abnormal. Some friends though Julie was weird while other friends just thought she was a wee bit different. The same holds true for her family who see her differently in different situations. The answer to the question of whether or not she needs professional help is a resounding "yes." Julie meets my two criteria which include behavior very much different from the norm and behavior that is negatively impinging on her life.

A few facts about OCD that are relevant to Julie's case relates to the time it has taken her to reach her current level of pathology. In future sessions, we found that her OCD characteristics could be seen as early as elementary school and her full blown symptoms have been evident for more than ten years. There is a general rule of thumb in psychology that relates the time that symptoms have been evident to the time that might be needed to bring the individual back to a normal state. In short, the longer the behaviors have been evident, the more difficult to turn things around. In addition OCD is pervasive and tends to spread to other areas. For example, excessive hand washing may spread to excessive cleaning or a need to constantly clean out one's closets. In Julie's case, the behaviors had been evident a long time and had spread to multiple areas. At the age of thirty-one, Julie now had an OCD Personality Disorder and not a simple diagnosis of OCD. What this means is that she would have to learn to manage her symptoms to minimize their effect on her life. She would always display these OCD characteristics as a personality disorder is a long standing consistency of traits relatively unchanged over time.

What can we learn from this? We can learn not to judge people's behavior without knowing all of the circumstances regarding the individual and the specific situation. We can stop putting labels on people to compartmentalize them into categories that only serve to make us more comfortable. If you walk to a store in your neighborhood today and you see a sweaty naked man running down the street screaming at the top of his lungs would you think he was crazy? You know better.

7. WHAT WAS THAT ABOUT?

On October 11th in the year 2001, one of my patients uttered the simple phrase, "What was that about?" At that time, his utterance held no significant meaning for me. In ensuing years, I came to understand the importance of those simple words. Herb was a seventy four year old recently retired accountant who came to see me for what he called depression. Herb was a thoughtful, sincere conservative man who had lost his wife ten years before he came to seek help. At his age of seventy-four, he was very fit physically and his thinking processes appeared to be very much intact.

He was born during World War 2 into a family with six older sisters. During our sessions, he told me numerous horror stories about being raised as the youngest child by seven mothers. He felt he could never do anything right and sought approval from every one of his mothers. All seven of them. His father adopted a below the radar approach to life and would constantly complain that since he couldn't get a word in edgewise, he was better off just keeping his mouth shut. Herb learned started copying this behavior at a very early age. Essentially, how to be mute. He married when he was twenty six to a woman with similar characteristics regarding her own introversion. Herb told me of numerous periods of time where they would go for days on end without speaking a word. No anger. No emotional games. Just a mutual desire not to communicate on any level. They decided, not surprisingly, to skip the whole raising child drama. The days just went on endlessly with the occasional vacation to Gettysburg during June (always in the month of June) at the same hotel and in the same room, if possible.

When Herb was thirty or thereabouts, he met a woman named Nancy. Nancy worked in an office on the third floor of his building while he worked on the fifth floor. It seems that fate placed a coffee shop on the fourth floor just a short hop from them both. He had noticed her for some time but knew that conversation was not his thing. At best, he could stutter through an inane conversation about the weather or the horrible traffic. One day, while he was sipping his Earl Grey, she sat down in the only available seat, directly across from him. Indeed, they conversed about the weather and the lousy traffic but something snapped way down in his psyche during that momentous lunch. He told me that, at the time, he really had no idea what was happening to him but that he felt different. For a few weeks, they met for lunch every day until Nancy suggested that they meet during their morning and afternoon breaks. Needless to say, Herb was thrilled with the additional meetings. But, he still couldn't explain what was going on.

During these weeks, Herb found himself very eager to get to work in the morning and reluctant to leave the building at the end of the day. He bought new clothes, began to wear cologne and started to, God help him, whistle. He became a whistling demon and found himself whistling on the street, while working and in the shower. He became a shower Pavarotti, bellowing catchy finger snapping tunes from Aida. Of course, after a few week, his wife noticed the major difference in his behavior but attributed his good cheer to the new quarterly edition of Accounting Today that had been delivered. Neither of them had the slightest clue as to what was happening to him but he was definitely morphing.

Nancy was in a loveless marriage with an insensitive and uncaring, wealthy man. Her husband had inherited a large furniture company and he spent the bulk of his time and energy on the business. She was becoming more and more unhappy and found Herb to be a great distraction as he let her talk for as long as she chose to ramble on. She found herself lingering after work and getting to work early every day. She purchased new clothes, had her hair done, tweezed her eyebrows, and started, as you can imagine, whistling. It's obvious where this is headed but both Herb and Nancy didn't have a clue.

After a few months of pure unadulterated, safe bliss, the eventual topic of meeting after work came up. Within a few weeks, they started drinking Pinot Noir or an occasional bottle of Cava in bistro surroundings that were totally alien to them. Nancy had no difficulty with her husband. He was just as happy with her out of the house. Herb, however, had to construct an elaborate series of lies to explain his late afternoon and early evening absences. Finally, after six months, Nancy decided that she wanted more. Much more. She wanted a wanton weekend away with Herb as long as it wasn't in Gettysburg.

That was when everything went wrong for the both of them. Nancy was more than ready to move on to a more intimate physical relationship while Herb was stuck in a novel situation without a guidebook. He simply didn't know what to do with all his conflicting emotions. On the one hand, he recognized the sexual attraction and desired stark-naked romps in motel rooms, beaches or any place Nancy wanted. He just couldn't do it without talking to his wife first about his feelings, something he had always been incapable of doing. He toyed with the idea for weeks and the weeks turned into months until Nancy gave him an ultimatum. Either have a real intimate sexual affair or end the relationship. He was able to string her along for a few more months until one day she stopped coming for their usual lunch get-togethers. At about the same time, she stopped meeting him for their breaks, both morning and afternoon. Distraught but still unable to deal with the situation, the whistling stopped as did the cologne and the debonair attitude. He would still arrive early and leave late with the hopes of running into her but she was under the radar for months. One day, taking a despondent late lunch, he saw Nancy at their table with one of the account executives. Unable to eat, he left the room and tried to figure out a way to rekindle their relationship. During the ensuing months, when he was able to accidentally run into her, he was unable to say the words he wanted to say. After a few months, she was always either in a hurry or late for a meeting and had no time for an exchange of any kind. Eventually, Herb reverted back to his old non-verbal ways but Nancy never left his memory. He would ruminate about her for years. Forty-four years to be exact. Why was he so paralyzed? Why couldn't he address the real issue which was his unhappy marriage? Could it have been because of his sisters, his father or his inherent lack of pluck. We will never really know and actually it's not important to figure out the source of the problem. What is important is to understand why he did not reassess his life and at least try to make some changes. When he asked me, "What was that about?", he was talking about his entire life and not just his short-lived flirtation with Nancy. It wasn't just the forty-four years thinking of Nancy and never taking any steps towards fulfillment, never taking stock of his life.

When I was growing up in New York, we had a phrase called a "do over." If you were playing stickball in the street, swinging your bat and a car came by very fast and interfered with your swing you could call a "do over" and you were able to swing again. If you were about to throw a football and just then a pit bull attacked you then you were entitled to a "do over." Unfortunately, there are very, very few "do overs" in real life. Usually, you are given one chance and once that moment has passed, your chances are gone. If you compound this by repeating the same mistake over and over your, chances of happiness and fulfillment are very small. Change is very difficult for many people but it is this fear that paralyzes us and makes us repeat the same negative patterns over and over and over and... You get the idea. Herb is the poster boy for an individual lacking the ability to introspect. However let me introduce you to Gina.

Gina was a married fifty one year old woman living in a very prestigious housing enclave in Florida. She had been married for about thirty years and told me that she felt lost. She and her husband had raised two children who were both recent college graduates and living out of state. Gina had noticed major changes in her husband's personality going back more than ten years. He became more and more reclusive after leaving his woodworking job to sit at home and stare at the trees in the backyard. When this happened Gina decided, out of spite, to leave her career in real estate to watch her husband stare at the trees. Possibility not the best idea and definitely not a proactive move motivated by a sense of spirituality and love. As time went on, the bills were paid on time every month out of a trust fund that Gina's parents setup. That trust fund was due to term out in about a year and there were no plans for the upcoming changes in their finances.

Gina reported that her husband became increasingly strange over the years and some of his behaviors had her concerned. His time in the backyard would begin at about eight in the morning and he would remain in one of his favorite chairs until sundown. Aside from a foray into the house for an occasional pee or a bag of chips he would simply sit and stare at the woods. In the home, he began to talk to the stuffed animals that their daughter had left behind when she went to college. Gina reported conversations lasting as long as two hours on a number of occasions. Her husband remained adamant in his refusal to seek help or to look for a job although Gina begged him to do something. The more he conversed with his stuffed animals and refused to work, the more she was determined not to be the one to go to work. This was a train wreck proceeding in slow motion down a track with a cliff at the end and a waterfall below the cliff. With their money lasting only another year and financial ruin staring them in the face she came for therapy. The problem was that Gina was not selfish enough. I'm aware that this sounds, on the surface, a little ridiculous but, in actuality, that was the problem.

When you fly on a commercial airline, the flight attendants always review the safety information and procedures for the passengers. When they talk about the oxygen masks dropping from above the seats, they make a point to put your own mask on first if you have a child sitting next to you. This sounds somewhat contradictory until you think it out. You need to take care of yourself before you are able to take care of someone else. I would imagine that if someone were observing this behavior, it might appear selfish when, in reality, it is the intelligent thing to do. In fact, there are two very different meanings for the word selfish. The first definition refers to an individual who is too concerned with one's own welfare while having little or no concern for others. The other much less known definition refers to an individual who is prompted by self-interest and advocates for oneself. It is a process where you take care of yourself first, not to the detriment of anyone else, but to simply make sure that you are intact and in control. Gina is a perfect example of a woman who became enmeshed in someone else's pathology and lost her own way. With financial impoverishment knocking on her front door she realized what she had done to herself by refusing to find meaningful employment. She also appreciated the hard fact that there was something terribly wrong with her husband.

What can we take away from the Gina and husband debacle? First, life does not grant many "do overs' so it is incumbent on each of us to use our time wisely. Ten years of watching a man stare into the woods to the detriment of both individuals is not something that can be undone. Second, life is not a rehearsal. We do not come back and undo the things we've done that have led us astray. Unless you're a cat, you have one shot and one shot only. Finally, you make your own luck. Gina constantly referred to the fact that she was unlucky but I disagree. Had she been proactive and dealt with the difficulties in an adult manner perhaps her "luck" would have been different. You never want to hear yourself say, "What was that about?"

8. HE'S NOT MUCH TO LOOK AT, BUT HE'S GOT A GREAT PERSONALITY

A number of years ago, one of my female patients, a woman age twenty-two, complained to me that most people were jealous assholes. Asking her to explain what she meant, she told me that an example would clarify it all. Recently, she had gone to a club in her area for a night out on the town. She went with a female friend because she would never go to a singles bar alone as going alone was just too tacky. When she walked into the club, she noticed a good many people looking at both her and her girlfriend and then turning away. Her explanation for their behavior was the simple fact that, when they looked at her they became extremely jealous. Furthermore, throughout the entire evening, not one individual, male or female, approached them to talk. She left the club with the firm conviction that the men in the club were morons and that they were intimidated by her looks. She believed that this happened to her a lot and that it was like having a curse that she would have to live with. It was to be her burden in life, to carry the cross of beauty wherever she would go.

Here's the problem. She was, by any definition, not as attractive as she believed she was. I'm being kind by saying that, in a purely physical manner, she was, at best, a four out of ten.

Again, I'm trying to be kind but the reality of what she saw and what everyone was able to see was, in fact, polar opposites. And yes, I know all that dribble about beauty being in the eye of the beholder. But, in her case, it would be difficult and totally unrealistic to buy into the fact that she was as gorgeous as she believed she was. How does someone manage to obtain such a false perception about their looks and personality?

Before we look at ways to explain her behavior, let's look at a twenty eight year old man that I saw at about the same time. Cornell was six feet tall with piercing blue eyes, great hair, perfect teeth and a smile that could even make Richard Nixon smile. In addition, he was a really terrific guy with a sense of spirituality and a concern for others. Cornell could not imagine himself as good looking as he truly was. He saw himself as an average guy with basically average looks.

So, what's going on here? How do we misperceive ourselves to such a degree? It all stems from our individual personality- the long standing characteristics of an individual that remains relatively consistent over time. Every personality is different- totally unique. There are no identical personalities even in identical twins. So, how do we get this unique set of traits that we carry with us through our lives?

The real answer, the honest truth, is that we really have no idea. Of course, there are numerous theorists who can write endless theoretical propositions. But, in fact, no one really knows. Sure, we know about Freud and Jung and Erikson. We also know about childhood experiences. But, we do not know why, for example, two children raised in the same household could have such different personalities. We don't know why one statement made to a child when in the third grade will reverberate with him throughout his entire life. We don't know why a rejection by a 16 year old girl will send some adolescent boys into a tailspin while others will simply profess that there are thousands of girls out there so why sweat. Why do I remember my high school counselor telling me that my future lies in the art world after I told him that I wanted to be an architectural engineer. I remember no other conversations when I was a junior in high school with the exception of a twenty minute talk with a counselor. What's that all about? So, the question remains, if personality is an enduring and consistent set of traits, can we really change?

The answer is yes and no. I had a female friend when I was eighteen. We would hang out together for hours on end. She was seventeen at the time. She was shy and reticent with little or no eye contact in her interactions with other people. People knew her as the nice quiet kid who wouldn't talk unless she had to. Physically, she was average, a little overweight and in dire need of a hair stylist. Very few people really knew her but those that did, including me, thought she was awesome. At the end of her junior year in high school she announced that she was leaving to go to her aunt's house in Seattle for her final year. Her move didn't make any sense to me at the time. I thought that there may be another reason for the move but I couldn't figure out what it could be. We kept in touch for over a year until she said that she'd be returning and asked me to pick her up at the airport. Waiting for flight 227 at Kennedy was painful. They appeared to unload more than a thousand people from that one flight. I never saw her come off the plane but I did see an absolutely gorgeous, outgoing, effervescent beauty of a woman chatting up the pilots. Again, you know where this is going. This was not the same young woman from a year ago. Her looks, her personality, her entire aura was changed. It seems that she was unhappy with what she had become and decided to reboot and become a different person both on the outside and the inside. To say that I was shocked would be a gross understatement as the change was profound. We hung around a lot during those first few weeks and we both discovered that while there was an apparent change in just about everything, she was basically the same person underneath. Conditions and changing situations can have a modifying effect on what appears to be a relatively stable set of traits. So, can you change? Once again, the answer is yes and no. If you're anal retentive and have devoted your life to frugality, neatness and cheapness that's just who you are and who you'll remain. The best theory explaining just how we form our personality is based on your interaction with others.

I won't bore you with the specifics but the theory has four parts. Number one is how you perceive yourself as if you're looking in a mirror. Not just the physical perception but also the entire personality. Two is related to how accurate your perception is as you take a good look at yourself. Number three has to do with how other people see you and react to you. Number four is just how different your self-perception is compared to how other might perceive you. All the perceptions should be somewhat in line. Unfortunately, many times, they are totally discordant. The previously mentioned twenty-two year old woman who thought that everyone was jealous of her is a perfect example of misperception.

Another thing about observing personalities that one should always keep in mind is to always listen to what people say about themselves. It would seem like a no brainer as we all think we listen to what people say about themselves. Barry, a friend of mine, who is not a patient, told me a story that makes a very important point. Barry was employed in a position that he enjoyed making more money than he had ever made before. Unfortunately, he had a friend Denny who made an outstanding offer of employment which was hard to turn down. Barry and Denny were good friends. They played basketball together on Sundays and pinochle on Thursday nights. They would go out to eat with their respective wives on occasion. In general, they got along very well. Denny had an enormous amount of money due to his father's hard work when he arrived in the States as an immigrant. In addition, Denny's older brother seemed to have a knack for making money. He was as cold as a fish but he was successful. Denny had no real history of success in business and was basically riding the wave of affluence.

When the negotiations for the position were nearing

an end, Denny told my friend that he could be somewhat difficult to work for and, at times, he could be a "prick." Barry heard these words and decided to go ahead with the deal anyways. Shortly after he started work, the difficulties began in earnest. Every two weeks, Barry would have to travel forty five minutes to go to Denny's office where he had to wait for his paycheck. He always had to wait for his expenses to be paid and money was an ongoing annoying problem.

He found out that Denny was a little man with a sizable ego who resented other people having more than he did. More than anything, he resented people who were happier than he was. Over the next two years, Barry realized that something was very wrong with his marriage. It seemed to be sliding rapidly downhill. He hired a detective. Sure enough, his boss and good friend was having an affair with his wife. In a way, this was not too upsetting as Barry was looking to get a divorce anyways and Denny's behavior only played into his overall plans. Fast forward a year and my friend was divorced and dating a very popular and attractive newly divorced woman living in the same town.

The final straw broke one Friday night when Denny called this woman at her home. Barry listened on the speaker phone to the entire conversation. Denny repeatedly told this woman that they were made for each other sexually and that he would continue to pursue her until she gave in. The entire conversation lasted ten minutes and Barry recorded the conversation on tape for future reference. A few days after the call, he had the opportunity to tell Denny exactly what he thought of him. Finally, he told him to take the job and stick it.

When Barry told me this story I asked him why he didn't go after Denny and destroy him. I confess that Barry is a much better person than I am but he let retribution go for three really good reasons. It seems that, despite the fact that Denny was an enormous prick, he was married to an exceptionally nice, kind and loving woman. They had two children. The woman and the two kids were the three reasons. The fact that Denny was a dick, by any measure in any universe, was an undeniable truth. But, why didn't my friend listen to the warning that he was given? Do we expect people to change for us? Do we think that they're not telling the truth? I think it has more to do with the fact that when someone admits something about themselves, they feel that behavior should be tolerated.

Let's say that you're at a meeting and the person sitting next to you is constantly fidgeting and making noises. Then, they lean over and say that they have ADHD and proceed, with pride, to be as annoying as possible. Another example is the man who tells his girlfriend that he has a wee bit of an anger problem. After his pronouncement, he feels justified with any aggressive behavior. After all, he told her that he had an anger problem. The examples are endless and they all point to the same thing. Expecting that your behavior is acceptable simply because you acknowledge that you have that behavior isn't okay.

What do we know now about our personality that we didn't know before reading this chapter? At this point, I'd say we have learned nothing but there is a way to open our eyes to ourselves. First, you need to stop doing whatever it is you're doing and take your emotional pulse. This is the right time to take a good look at oneself. Possibly for the first time. Make a list of ten characteristics that define who you are. Be brutally honest (more about this list later). Bounce this off your friends, family or anyone who can be honest with you. Evaluate your lifestyle. Evaluate your friends and family members. Evaluate your career. The next step is to change. It's really pretty easy... Take a good look... Evaluate... Decide to make some changes. In this process, you need to set some new realistic and achievable goals for the future. There will be much more on achieving goals in the next few chapters.

9. SHOULDN'T I BE HAPPIER THAN I AM?

I would like to invite you to a ritual that millions of people follow every morning. I would like you to get a cup of coffee or tea, find a comfortable place to sit and read today's local newspaper with me. Let's see what pleasantries are waiting to greet us.

- Persistent red tide takes toll as people postpone vacation plans... The red tide has devastated wildlife.
- Driver crashed, died of injuries... fleeing a police car.
- The U.S. has lost more troops to suicide than hostile activity over the course of a decade.
- Putnam and DeSantis slugged it out with one-liners for much of their hour long debate.
- Russia breached Florida's election systems... A continuance of pervasive acts to try to weaken and divide the United States.
- Rich Gates implicated the former Trump

campaign chairman and himself in financial crimes.

- California fire among the worst ever... blackened an area the size of Los Angeles.
- Eleven children found in a disheveled living compound where a man was training them to commit school shootings.
- Woman stopped for a DUI after describing herself as a "clean, thoroughbred, white girl" to escape charges from the police.
- Four Missouri children found in windowless rooms with no access to water or toilets.
- Venezuela top court orders lawmakers arrested after an alleged assassination attempt.
- Nikolas Cruz, who killed 17 people in Marjorie Douglas High School, claims a demonic voice in his head urged him "to do violence."
- Dolphins found dead near Venice, Florida because of the red tide.
- Charlottesville gave momentum to Confederate monument foes... The deadly violence that rocked the town a year ago.
- Voting rights to former felons?
- Prepare for hurricane season... Storms last year caused more than 460 deaths and at least 316 billion dollars in damages
- Cruelty towards immigrants... A Federal judge ordered
- U.S. government officials to stop administering psychotropic medication to migrant children without parental consent.

- Possible constitutional right to bear arms in public to be considered
- Democrats dangerous rhetoric... Carlos Bayan was arrested after leaving threatening messages promising to go after 2 politicians and "feed them lead."
- Climate change... This is a huge problem for our area.
- State Representative Newton is being criticized for taking money from special interests.
- Calls to repeal "stand your ground" reach the Capitol... Tensions over the July 19th shooting of twenty eight year old Markeis McGlockton.
- Local home prices lag behind the State.
- Immigration raids in Nebraska target businesses
- German pilots join Ryanair strike forcing 400 flights to be canceled
- Buy stocks or miss out... Investors missing out as they shed stocks.
- Then, you can read Dear Anne or Dear Annie to learn about a multitude of dysfunctional behaviors. Now, go to the health column and read about the risks associated with a tonsillectomy. On to sports...
- Winston lets Bucs down with his three game suspension.
- Braden River high school sanctioned... Two students received impermissible benefits by living with families of current student athletes.
- Red tide (once again) bloom keeps spreading...

The red scourge arrived on our shores."

Now let's take a peek at your horoscope where you will find a number of statements totally unrelated to you and your life. I would suggest you not read the five full page ads for hearing aids as this will definitely depress you. Finally, let's check the obituaries to see if you know anyone who has passed and to also make sure that the preponderance of people dying are at least your age or older.

Put your chai tea down and think about the roughly thirty-four negative issues that are floating around in your head. How can you transition from all that negativity to a good day? Why do we choose to sabotage ourselves with information that has very little bearing on our lives? Why has happiness taken a back seat to turmoil and negativity?

I have been accused in the past of being too happy. In fact, when I heard this from others I began to believe that there might be something wrong with me. In retrospect, I think they had it all wrong and I've been on the right track. Happiness, like beauty, is in the eye of the beholder. It is a concept that is difficult to define as it differs from situation to situation.

The New Yorker magazine once published a cartoon showing all members of an audience watching a play and crying. Smack dab in the middle of the group was a man with a gigantic grin on his face. Why and how did he see humor while everyone else was saddened by what they saw? Happiness suggests a feeling of great pleasure or contentment. The man in the theater saw something that directly related to him and made him happy. Contentment is another animal altogether, It refers to having no desire for anything more or different. Imagine living a life where you have no desire for more. Another way of looking at this is to answer the question "when is enough, enough?"

I believe that, in order to reach the contentment goal, you must first live in your own reality. I would have liked, at least once in my life, to dunk a basketball. Given my height and athletic ability, this is something that has never happened. Nor will happen in the distant future. I easily came to grips with that in the seventh grade when I stood next to George who was already six foot three inches tall. I also know that I will never play the guitar, violin, piano, accordion or any instrument that requires my brain to move my fingers in a coordinated fashion. This is never going to happen as my fingers and my brain are disconnected. What we need to do is to know our strengths and weaknesses so that we can save ourselves future grief and embarrassment. Should Eric Clapton bang on my front door and offer to give me free guitar lessons. I would have to decline to save both of us a good deal of frustration and disappointment.

In addition to getting a realistic picture of yourself, there are two more concepts that can help you on your way to Nirvana. First you would need to develop an appreciation for life and whatever is in your own personal universe. One of the truisms in life is that everything is relative. If you keep comparing what your life is with others, eventually you will lose this ridiculous contest. If you have a great house, someone else will have a bigger, more expensive home. If you think your boat is truly spiffy, wait until you pull up next to a boat that is fifty feet longer. There's a quote out there that says that wanting what you don't have diminishes what you do have.

Finally, be grateful. We all need to express gratitude and thankfulness. Even if things occasionally hit the proverbial fan, which they will at times. I visited a friend of mine in the hospital years ago. My friend, Nancy, had a leg badly affected by polio when she was a child. As a result, she walked with a noticeable limp and was unable to partake in most physical activities. She called the impaired leg her "bad leg" and the other leg was the "good leg." Never once in the forty odd years that I knew her did she complain about her leg, her pain or the limitations that her "bad leg" imposed on her. Unfortunately, Nancy was diabetic and needed an operation to remove her leg. In a strange twist of fate and irony she had to have her "good leg" removed. I visited her shortly after the operation and had no idea as to what to say. I felt that I could commiserate and tell her what a cruel stroke of fate she has endured, but in reality I had no idea what to say. After the initial hellos, Nancy just looked down at her remaining leg and said, "I never thought I'd be calling this my good leg." That's the way she was, taking life as it was dealt and being grateful for what she had. I wish I could be more like her. I really believe that we'd all be better off if we just looked around with some appreciation for what we have and stop complaining about what's missing in our lives.

I have a question for you. What would make you happy? Think about both short term happiness and long term happiness, and try to be as realistic as you can be. We're not talking about winning the lottery or finding jewels in your backyard. In your realistic world, what can you do to bring a little more joy into your life? Then, try to figure out the answer to the larger Nike question. Why can't you just do it?

A number of years ago, I had a seventy year old patient who we'll call Mr. M. After our introductions, I explained the therapy process as best as I could. After the explanation, he told his story.

"When I came to this country from Italy, I was only seventeen and didn't speak more than twenty or thirty words of English. I could ask for the bathroom and maybe order a pizza. But, that was about it. There were a great number of embarrassing times due to my lack of English. My parents were hard workers and they both had jobs in the garment center in New York. They would leave every day at seven in the morning and get home at about seven at night. They did this six days a week. The weekends served to catch up on what couldn't be done during the week. Watching them struggle I decided that I would have my own business and I would be successful beyond my wildest dreams. I was willing to work, but not for someone else. If I was to put in sixty or seventy hours a week, I would do it for myself and not have to answer to anyone else.

I was very fortunate to have made friends with a group of people who recently moved to New York from Northern Italy and wanted what I was looking for in my new life. Nicky, my new friend, told me about an opportunity in the Bronx selling fruits and vegetables in a wholesale market. We formed a partnership and began to work together selling to restaurants in New York. Then in New Jersey.

Then, the entire east coast as far south as Georgia. We seemed to have a knack for what we were doing and were wildly successful far exceeding our initial goals. During this time, I married and had two daughters who both set up businesses similar to mine. They have also been successful.

By now, you're probably wondering why I decided to come to therapy and bare my soul. On the surface, everything looks good, really good. We have a giant house in Upper Saddle River, New Jersey and another house in upstate New York that we use during the summer and the holidays. I have four grandchildren and my health is fine. I guess the problems started when my friend and partner Nicky got very sick a number of years ago. After a horrible six years of cancer treatment, he died. I went into a major funk and hit rock bottom. If I were a drinker, I probably would have been drinking every day. If I were a druggie, I would have probably self-medicated myself so I wouldn't feel any pain. The problem was that I had no way to cope with the loss. Then the questions started coming.

I started to question what life was all about and if there was a purpose to all this craziness we call life? I started to think about my life and was not happy with anything that I saw. Work has always been my number one priority with family a close second. Now, it all seems senseless. You would expect a man with more than thirty five million dollars in assets to be the happiest man on the planet but I'm far from being that person.

One of my daughters is as cold as ice. She acts more like a robot with no true feelings. My other daughter has gone to the best private schools and now has a shitty attitude that turns everyone off. My wife and I have a very easy platonic relationship with absolutely no passion. The only passion I ever see in her is when she sits down to a good plate of linguini and clam sauce. But, she's not the problem and I know that. It's just that my life holds no happiness and every day feels the same like that movie Groundhog Day"

Before the session came to an end, we talked a great deal about his upbringing, his family and the loss of Nicky. We scheduled an appointment for the next week and I deliberately did not give him any solutions to his difficulties as I needed to sort through my notes and come up with a treatment plan. I'm sure that other therapists would have immediately referred him to a psychiatrist for medications that would only mask the true difficulties.

Mr. M showed up on time for his next session and after the usual inane conversation about the weather, I simply asked him what would make him happy. He didn't respond. I repeated the question as I wasn't sure that he heard me the first time. He told me that he had no idea as to what would make him truly happy. It was something that he never thought about because the concept of happy was out of his conscious realm. Needless to say, he struggled for a while with this new strange and mysterious concept until a little smile formed on his lips. I knew then that he was on the right track and was thinking outside of his usual box. Finally, he told me that he wanted to buy a Rolls Royce. I asked him if he had the funds and he said yes. Then, he told me that his two daughters would think that he was losing his mind. He told me about his dream to take the Concorde to Paris for an overnight and eat at the best restaurants in the city. Once again his only fear was the negative feedback from his daughters. But, then, he said that it would be their problem. Not his. As he was about to leave, he looked at me, told me that what he would most like to do is donate money to The National Italian American Foundation and help people who have fallen on hard times. Every year, the Foundation has a dinner and people openly pledge their dollars for the cause. Last year, actually every year, he donated ten thousand dollars and everyone clapped and applauded and he felt really proud of himself. This year, he was thinking of giving a million dollars. "Why wouldn't I? I have it. I can spend it as I like and I'm just going to do it."

I was a bit shocked by this statement and, in a weird way, felt responsible for having this man donate such a large sum of money. I didn't see Mr. M for two weeks because he called to tell me he would be out of town. When he was due for his next session, he called and asked me to meet him outside of my office. There he stood next to a beautiful brand new Rolls Royce. He was beaming as if he just hit his first Little League home run. We went into my office and I asked him about his recent trip out of town. He gave me a sly smile and said, "I'll bet you can guess where I went." I took a wild guess and blurted out "Paris." He just smiled and shook his head. He told me that he took his wife away for three nights to the best hotels and restaurants and had a fantastic time. Hearing about this trip, I began to think of the million dollar donation he said that he wanted to make. So. I asked. He said," No. No. No. I didn't give a million dollars because I sat down with my accountant to review my finances and I found that I could give two million, which I did." To say that I was stunned would be a gross understatement. I sat there, almost unable to speak for a few seconds. He told me that his daughters were seriously taken aback and were starting to question his sanity probably to make sure that he didn't dispose of any more of his assets.

To some people, Mr. M's spending to be happy would appear to be shallow and frivolous. To others, it may appear that he is a happy kind man disposing of his assets in a way that makes him happy. The point is that "happy" differs from person to person and is dependent upon the unique situation and the players involved.

As I've said before, happiness is in the eye of the beholder. What food makes you happy? In my case, my wife's homemade lasagna brings a smile to my face and a slight drool to my lips. What food makes you happy? How much money do you feel you need to be happy? For some people, they never seem to accumulate enough and will work extra years to build up a sum that they can never use because by the time they want to use it, they're too old.

How much sex do you need? Does once a week work for you? Or do you need to have sex every single day? With an odd day off here and there. How much love do you need? How much laughter do you need? You need to think hard about this and try to incorporate some happiness in your life while you still have a chance to accomplish some of your goals. Everyone should sit down and formulate a bucket list. Then, do what you can to make yourself happy. The sad fact is that if you don't do something, no one else will. The responsibility and the accountability is yours and yours alone.

10. AM I ALLOWED TO DRINK WITH MY MEDICATION?

One of the most interesting specialties a therapist can choose when practicing psychotherapy is couple's counseling. Many people refer to this as marriage counseling and believe that the goal of therapy is to ensure that the two individuals involved walk off into the sunset, holding hands to live happily ever after with the sound of little birds chirping love songs on their shoulders. My belief is that this should not be the goal. From my perspective, my job as a therapist is to have the couple take a good look at their relationship and attempt to change what isn't working. Then, they should make an honest assessment of the state of their marriage. Sometimes, people actually are not right for each other and they need to plan for a different future with a different soul mate. What is also very perplexing is how the husband and wife view themselves and their partner in the relationship.

Byron was a thirty eight year old family law attorney. He called to set up an appointment to discuss some significant marital discord. Initially, he wanted to come in with his wife for the sessions but I told him that I like to see the patients individually first. I have seen too many sessions turn into total chaos as the parties vie for power. Byron presented as a very handsome, gregarious and very charismatic man. Wearing a traditional, three-piece lawyer suit, he presented his case as if he were in court presenting a case to a jury. The following will give you an idea as to how the session transpired.

"This coming June we'll be married for 17 years. I met my wife Cassidy when we were both seniors at L.S.U. In the fall of that year. We were married at the end of the next year when we were both in law school at Georgetown. Cassidy breezed through law school as if were the easiest thing in the world while I had to study twice as hard to get the same grades. She is a very, very bright, beautiful and capable woman who everyone seems to love. I mean, I think I'm likable. But she's just off the charts. We have three children ages six, nine and eleven. They all go to private schools. Financially, we are blessed with incomes that allow us to not be concerned about finances. We've already made long term plans to retire at the age of fifty.

We have a beautiful home and late model cars. On the surface, we're the ideal couple. We work in the same office. I work three full days a week while Cassidy works four days a week. Unfortunately, what lurks below is a different matter altogether. I know that as a therapist, there are things that you're looking for so let me take care of some of the more delicate questions. First of all, our sex life is wonderful. No problems in that area whatsoever. Secondly, there is no drama related to either of us having an affair, thinking of an affair or anything related to infidelity. Thirdly there are no family members tearing us apart. No horrible in-law stories, druggie cousins or schizophrenic aunts or uncles. Financially, as I said, we're more than fine. In addition, there is no problem with a whole slew of other difficulties that must plague other couples.

I believe our particular problems began when I met her in college. Her father was a teaching P.G.A pro who had been teaching golf for years at a private club. Cassidy started to play when she was ten and was really good. When I met her, she had already won a number of minor amateur tournaments. Her mantra when it came to golf was, "Practice, practice, practice." She would play every weekend and would go to the range two or three nights a week. For the first few years, this was our life. I adjusted my schedule around her golf schedule. As the years went by, her game stabilized and she hit a plateau as an excellent club player but the P.G.A. tour was acknowledged as being out of her reach. We settled into a somewhat irregular routine where time was always made for golf. So, what the heck does golf have to do with my being here? Actually, it's much more than that.

I need to man up and tell you what my life has become. Before I do that, I have to confess that, as a lawyer, I am totally unable to present this case to my wife. She is so incredibly bright verbally that any time I try to express my concerns to her, she gives me her arguments which, in reality, make me feel like an idiot. No matter how prepared I am to discuss my feelings and no matter how long I wait for the right moment, it never seems to work because she immediately throws me off track.

I've turned into one of those mother types who worry about everything. I've become a bit of a wreck and my anxiety is starting to interfere with my life at home, in the office and with friends and family. I have become the traditional woman in the marriage and the total role reversal has me tied in knots. I take care of the three kids. I pack their lunch, I help them with their homework, special assignments and school projects. I have made at least four spurting volcanoes in the last six years for my kids. I drive them to school and I make the sitter arrangements to have them picked up. I do the house cleaning and straightening up. Even though we have a woman in to clean twice a week, the house still needs a great deal of work. I do the laundry every day. I take care of the shopping, which is beginning to become a monumental task.

I also make all the vacation plans for the family as well as plans involving our mutual families. Thanksgiving and Christmas are always solely my responsibility including a sit down dinner for thirty people. The only people missing are Native Americans. Otherwise, it's a feast for all who attend. I set up the doctor and dental appointments, play dates and sleepovers for the kids. She openly admits that she has no maternal instincts as if by saying this it makes it okay.

Although there is much more, the final issue is the fact that I handle all the money. I pay all the bills, make all the transfers, check our savings accounts and keep track of our annuities. She has no concern whatsoever for our finances nor does she understand how hard it is to keep track of our money due to her constant spending. As I've said, there's a great deal more. The real question is how in God's name did we ever evolve into this one sided allocation of responsibilities? I have no idea.

So, how did this all come to a head? There are a number of things that have happened in the past few months that have opened my eyes. I have been slipping a bit at work and I believe that the staff is beginning to notice. I sleep poorly and wake up at five to start doing the laundry. I work with the kids after supper and finally put them to bed at about nine so that by the time I get to bed, it's usually ten or so and my mind is spinning. As a result, I usually fall asleep at around twelve.

Cassidy still plays golf every Sunday. Most weekends, she plays on Saturday also. She goes to the driving range once or twice during the week as she has always done and, in a rare moment of weakness, she will actually sit down with one of the kids and help with their homework. And now for the straw that broke the camel's back. Every year, she goes with her girlfriends on golfing vacations that last anywhere from a weekend to a full week. We never discuss her going away because it is expected that I will take care of things while she is away.

About six weeks ago, I tried, once again, to talk to her about my being overwhelmed and about my anxiety level getting to a point where it was interfering with my life. As usual, she made me feel that all the problems were minimal and that the difficulty was my inability to multitask effectively. She completely deflected my concerns and, once again, felt that she was entitled to lead her life because that's the way we've always done things. I was so frustrated and angry that I wanted to lash out and hit something. Not someone. Something. Fortunately, my strong Christian ethic kicked in and I just got quiet and I now understand that my silent behavior has not served me well.

Cassidy told me that, in a month, she was leaving for a ten day golf outing in Phoenix. No discussion. No conversation. Just a flat out statement of fact announcing her upcoming departure. That's when I lost it and said, "Who the fuck do you think you are? Do you think you can just dictate where the fuck you go when it suits you? There's something the fuck wrong with you. Fuck you, fuck you to hell." I have never cursed like that in my life. I think that I was more surprised that she was. Maybe I had watched too many Soprano re-runs. I really don't know. I left the house and took a two hour walk to cool down because I was upset with what I had said. When I walked in I thought that I had cooled down until she smiled at me as if I was an idiot and asked, "Are you over your little tirade now?" There is no doubt that there is something wrong with this whole picture. I'm afraid that if we don't make some major changes then we will be seeking our own attorney. First, I need to do something about my anxiety which is crippling me and stops me from being able to deal with Cassidy's verbal manipulations. So whaddya think?"

Byron had been living with an anxiety coping disorder and was unable to think and process clearly enough for us to take steps to deal with his situation. I recommended a psychiatrist that I had worked with in the past. She was not the traditional psychiatrist as her views on medication were almost as negative as mine. Never, in all the years I worked with her, did she over-medicate or immediately prescribe meds.

We both held the belief that, in most cases, medication should be prescribed in order to facilitate therapy. The medication should serve to calm the patient down and allow him to gain insight into the difficulties. Only then could therapy proceed successfully and with a chance of a good result. Patients who have been taking Prozac, Xanax or a slew of other meds for years have masked their symptoms and are no closer to a cure than they were when they started meds. With this in mind, we began a total of six months of meds with therapy weekly for Byron. The one question Byron asked was, "Am I allowed to have a drink or two with my meds?" In the past, it seems that he had been self-medicating with copious amounts of Sauvignon Blanc to get through the day. I suggested that he switch to iced tea for the upcoming six months or so.

While Byron was coming in once a week and adjusting to his medication I began to see Cassidy. She was, as Byron had stated, breathtaking in every sense of the word. From the top of her perfectly coiffed hair to the bottom of her expensive four inch heels, she was perfect. Even her teeth were so snow-white and perfect that she could have easily been a toothpaste model. Blonde and beautiful, that's all I kept thinking. Blonde and beautiful. She was, from the onset outgoing, verbal, intimidating and astonishingly manipulative. Cassidy was a woman who actually demanded the superior role in any relationship.

Here are some statements that Cassidy made during our sessions that give a glimpse into her personality:

"So, you're the guy who's going to straighten out my husband, Good luck."

"You're probably going to have to give Byron a hell of a lot more drugs to just stop him from whining."

"He complains about taking care of the kids like that's some big deal. They're kids for God's sake and he's supposed to be the adult."

"Money has never been an issue for me. I spend what I want and all he does is complain. If I have to account to anyone then why do I work?"

"Golf is important to me. Very important. I believe that a husband has an obligation to support their spouse. So, I play a good deal of golf and that's the way it's always been, and always will be until I die."

"Tell me how a man can complain about anything if he only works three days a week while I work four. I should be the one complaining instead of him but he's relentless in trying to talk to me about his poor over-worked life."

"Everyone I know is aware of the fact that I am a "fun" person. I'm not built for the daily household crap, being maternal and all that other stuff people seem to love. I'm the same way with family, friends and acquaintances. I'm the person at the party having fun while other people worry and concern themselves with inconsequential trivial rubbish"

"The odds of fixing him are about the same as the odds of getting hit by lightning."

There were many more of these statements and all

were in the same negative vein. Here was a woman with a remarkable lack of empathy, a lack of maternal feelings whatsoever and an inability to see that she and her marriage were sliding downhill fast. Sessions with Cassidy were always difficult. She was unable to see the situation from any perspective but her own. But that was all about to change.

Byron was growing by leaps and bounds. His therapy was progressing beyond our wildest imagination. We discussed his childhood and the effect it had on his behavior. We labored to understand Cassidy and her behavior until one day he had what we call an "aha" experience. He was able to see clearly for the first time that the problem was not his and his alone. He realized the role that Cassidy had played over the years and finally understood how his life became what it had become. He could see beyond Cassidy's beauty, brains and fun personality and see that she very was far from perfect with a whole set of her own complex problems.

After about ten weeks, I was able to schedule the two of them together. In order to manage Cassidy's steamrolling personality, I incorporated a number of rules into our mutual sessions. The first rule is what I call the Navajo way. This is a simple conversational rule that is extremely difficult for some people and simple for others. In the Navajo way, you never interrupt a person when they are talking. That "never" is absolute. Even if the other individual is lying, cursing or screaming, you are bound by this rule. You have to sit and wait for your chance to speak.

The second part of this process is actually the most

difficult. Whoever has the floor maintains the floor until he or she states that they are done. What this accomplishes is to allow an individual to speak without rushing and it further allows you to get all your thoughts out without being interrupted when you take a breath. Byron had no difficulty with this but Cassidy said that she felt bound and gagged. Nevertheless, therapy proceeded and Byron had the ability to speak his mind for the first time. The change was remarkable.

The power was shifted and the inequities were so blatant that they both realized that change was in the wind. This process was not easy for either of them but, in the long run, they persevered and saved their marriage. Cassidy even continued to see me after they stopped coming as a couple as it seems that she recognized her need to make some changes to be a wee bit happier (there's that happy word again). Cassidy needed to grow up a bit and lighten up on her need to be the fun person.

Byron regained his voice. Cassidy began to open up and truly modify her behavior. If this were a perfect ending then we would see them teeing off together three or four times a week with a golf cart specially made for them and the three kids. In this perfect world, everything would be glorious and Cassidy would be the mother of the year, supporting her husband and children on a daily basis. Byron would totally man-up and take an equal position with Cassidy.

Obviously, this did not happen as we all know that this is not a perfect world. People's lives are not what we see in Disney movies. They would struggle with the new roles and would have to make many mid-course corrections to maintain their marriage, which they did. Cassidy and Byron presented as most couples do, with totally different perspectives. If you want to see just how disparate views can be just talk to a divorce attorney or spend some time watching Jerry Springer.

I personally have very strong feelings with regard to medication and its overuse. I have met with individuals who come to me with as many as seven different medications. Five of which were specifically for mental disorders. Most patients inform me that they have been taking two or three medications for years. In 2016, 338 million prescriptions were written for anti-depressants alone. There are also anti-anxiety meds, stimulants, mood stabilizers and anti-psychotic medications.

Some of the more popular of the above meds are Celexa, Lexapro, Prozac, Luvox, Paxil, Wellbutrin, Effexor, Concerta and, the most widely prescribed drug, Zoloft. Let's take a minute to look at the possible side effects of the most widely prescribed medication. Let's say you're battling some depression and you start a prescription for Zoloft. The possible side effects are sleepiness, drowsiness, feeling tired, nervousness, insomnia, headache, stiff muscles, uneven heartbeat, memory problems, dizziness, nausea, skin rash, diarrhea, constipation, upset stomach, changes in appetite, abnormal ejaculation, impotence, decreased sex drive, difficulty having an orgasm, dry mouth and weight loss. The possible side effects appear to be more debilitating than the depression you are attempting to battle. To compound matters you may be prescribed two or more medications to battle your depression and the combined interactive effects of the two or three meds are, for the most part, almost impossible to predict.

Unless you're taking anti-psychotic meds or medication for acute symptoms, medication should be a relatively short term solution to your difficulties and should not become a part of your everyday life for the next twenty years. If you're one of those people who take three, or four, or five medications, you have effectively lost yourself in your medication nightmare and you have no idea as to who you truly are. Once on medication, your goal should be to see how quickly you can stop the meds and get on with your life. For some inexplicable reason, drug manufacturers are not too happy with me. But, as they say in the South, "It is what it is."

11. A PRIEST, A RABBI AND A NUN WALK INTO A BAR

Take a few moments, humor me, and read the following.

- I broke a mirror in my house and I'm supposed to get seven years bad luck. But, my lawyer thinks he can get me five.
- I can't listen to that much Wagner. I start getting the urge to conquer Poland.
- I believe there is something out there watching us. Unfortunately, it's the government.
- I called a wrong number today. I said, "Hello, is Joey there?" A woman answered and she said, "Yes he is.." Then I said, "Can I speak to him please?" She said, "No, he can't talk right now,. He's only two months old." I told her I'd wait.
- There were two peanuts walking down a dark alley, one was assaulted.
- Don't sweat the petty things and don't pet the sweaty things.

- Have you ever noticed that anybody driving slower than you is an idiot, and anyone going faster than you is a maniac?
- "I am" is reportedly the shortest sentence in the English language. Could it be that "I do" is the longest sentence?
- I bought a new dog. He's a paranoid retriever. He brings back everything because he's not sure what I threw him.
- I went to a tourist information booth and asked them to tell me about some tourists who were here last year.
- I'm not afraid of heights, I'm afraid of widths.
- How many Alzheimer's patients does it take to change a light bulb?... ..To get to the other side.
- What did one snowman say to the other? Nice balls.
- Why can't you hear a pterodactyl in the bathroom?
- Because it has a silent pee.
- I was thinking about how people seem to read the Bible a whole lot as they get older;. Then, it dawned on me. They are cramming for the final exam.
- I went to a bookstore and asked the saleswoman, "Where's the self-help section?" She said that if she told me, it would defeat the purpose.
- My parents got divorced. They had a custody fight over me. No one showed up.

Chances are that you found a few of these jokes mildly amusing. On the other hand, you probably found a number of these jokes to be stupid. Even offensive. Another person, very similar to you may have found them all hilarious while his best friend would think that they were all dated and totally boring. There are also those who would read these little jokes and find no humor in them whatsoever. I worry about joyless people.

Why the tremendous disparity in perception? We're all reading the same thing aren't we? The answer is that everyone's sense of humor is different, very much like our fingerprints or our personalities. Everyone is unique and different from every other person in a world filled with billions of people. Even identical twins will show marked personality differences and as a result, will see humor differently.

The real question that begs to be asked is when was the last time you laughed out loud? When was the last time you chuckled or guffawed at something seen or heard? How many years has it been since milk or soda squirted out of your nose? It's a question that needs to be asked. If you are unable to remember the last time you laughed, I worry about you also.

A laugh is defined as an explosive sound that expresses mirth, amusement or ridicule. In 1962, 95 of 192 students at a school in Tanzania experienced laughing attacks. It seems that, for some strange reason, the laughter became contagious and the students were unable to control their glee. The school was forced to close for a while until the raucous laughing ceased. Contrast this experience to a meeting of therapists, or attorneys, or funeral director's where there is not a single snigger to be found. Once again, humor is dependent on the particular situation, the other individuals present and a host of other factors. On the plus side, there has been a great deal of research on laughter and its effects. Laughter actually boosts immune functions, increases pain tolerance, improves cardiovascular health and memory...and that's no joke.

Humor is the quality that makes something seem funny, amusing or comical. Appropriate humor is very much like appropriate laughter and is dependent on numerous unique factors. Let's face it. There are people with absolutely no sense of humor. These are the people who seem to always tell you that they just don't get it when the joke is done. These are the same individuals who, after four glasses of wine, try to tell a joke. It never works out as their discomfort is evident throughout the telling of the joke. A comedian once said, when referring to individuals who were not very bright, that you "can't fix stupid." Humor is similar as you can't fix it. There's no pill. No amount of watching SNL will change the fact that if you don't already have a good sense of humor, you probably never will. Sad.

A number of years ago, a very sweet young lady named Elise came to see me. She was just eighteen and wanted to leave her house so badly that she was planning to run away. Primarily because of her father. Her father was an artist who had been raised by his parents after moving to the States from Bulgaria. He was raised in a very strict environment with rules for just about everything. He thought that it would only be right to have these rules for his family. I have listed some of the rules below as reported by Elise.

- The refrigerator door is never to be kept open more than ten seconds.
- Doors to the outside must never be open more than five seconds.
- The thermostat is never to be touched and will remain at eighty degrees throughout the year (in Florida).
- Vegetables and fruit will only be bought from the bins in the stores which sell for half price as they cannot be sold at full price.
- Lights and fans can only be on if you are in the room. When you leave the room, even for a few minutes you need to shut the fan and the light.
- When dining everyone would eat under a single forty watt bulb. All other lights must be off.
- Never pile dirty dishes on top of each other because, then, you have to wash the bottom side.
- Never shop without coupons and buy only what is on sale.
- Never touch the books in the bookcases.
- Never touch the stereo system or the cds.
- Never put the dog poop in the toilet. Always double wrap the cat turds in two separate bags.
- Never mix up the food in the refrigerator as there is a corresponding space on each shelf depending upon the food.

- Park the cars directly over the cardboard on the garage floor in case there is an oil leak.
- Never move the rags that are placed on the floor in the kitchen in case they're needed for a spill of any kind.

THIS LIST COULD BE MUCH LONGER as she mentioned at least fifteen or twenty other rules, all basically insignificant. The bottom line was that her father was totally controlling every aspect of her life. I asked her about her father's social skills. She said that he had none. I asked about his sense of humor. To no one's surprise, she said he had none. Elise went so far as to tell me that she couldn't remember a time when he laughed in the last five or ten years. A joyful soul he was not and, now, he was beginning to pay the price for his tight controls.

Elise also told me that her mother demanded that she and her husband go to counseling together due to his dictatorial personality. They found a therapist and went for five or six sessions a few months ago. Elise told me that at the end of the sixth session, the therapist fired himself. She also told me that her father was very enraged with the therapist and demanded an explanation for the firing. The therapist tried to explain the reasoning for the termination but was unable to get through to her father. There was no way to convince him to see the error of his ways and the need to change. Supposedly, when the therapist was pushed to the brink he reportedly told her father to "just fucking lighten up!"

I have no idea if those words were truly spoken but Elise and her mother now use that lighten up phrase as their mantra and repeated it to her dad every possible chance. It seems that he lost a great deal of his power along with his credibility which he was never able to recover. The question is not how he had come to be who he was. The real question is why someone would choose to live in a regimented world with an absence of joy despite the fact that his world was crumbling around him. Why couldn't he look at his life and decide to change and live a more fulfilling life with a few chortles along the way? There is no simple answer but the fact remains that we all have choices. He had decided to choose a lifestyle that most people would run away from. Had I been the father's therapist, I would have probably fired myself also to save both of us from a great deal of disappointment. I have my own set of rules.

In other instances, humor can work in overdrive and become a major personality disorder although there is no official DSM classification for over-humorizing. Izzy came to me with an initial complaint of social dysfunction. He told me that almost all of the people he knows are idiots, or assholes, or just plain stupid. Izzy was thirty-three and single. He had a long and very unsuccessful history of dating and settled for living with a dog, two cats and a goldfish. Average looking and well dressed, he always came to the sessions with a big smile on his face. He worked in a small accounting office with a staff of twelve and had been there for five years. He had no friends at the office. After a few sessions, it became apparent that his social dysfunction was brought about by his behavior and not due to the fact that "all people are jerks." Izzy had an inability to keep his mouth shut. He was a joke teller with a repertoire of hundreds or maybe thousands of jokes to tell. This, in itself doesn't, sound like a terrible affliction, but, as I've said before, the sheer volume of the jokes pushed him into the "abnormal' category.

What I was to find out along the way was the fact that Izzy had OCD as he was obsessed with telling jokes. He would enter the office, sit down and then tell me one or two jokes in quick succession. His modus operandi was to tell a few jokes quickly with the hopes that of the three or four jokes one would be minimally funny and he'd get a positive response. This one joke served as a catalyst for another slew of jokes and so on, and so on. There is a phrase in psychology called 'meaningful communication' which refers to a true understandable dialogue between two parties. In Izzy's case, there was no meaningful communication as thoughts were not exchanged and the dialogue was one-sided. To compound matters, Izzy felt a need to share his mirth with one and all. He would be asked numerous times by his co-workers to please stop telling his jokes to waiters and waitresses to no avail. To make matters even worse his banter, was childish and immature and repeated time after time to his office friends until they stopped going out to lunch with him. Hence, they became, in his eyes, idiots and jerks. Here are a few examples that will give you a better idea of his behavior. Upon sitting down at a table in a restaurant, the waiter would ask if there was a beverage they would like to order. Every time, Izzy would say that he didn't care for a beverage but could he have a coke. Funny? No. Amusing? No. Annoying? Absolutely! If the wait staff would ask if there's anything else they could do Izzy would say, "a massage would be nice." How many times can you hear these little quips before you wanted to pull your own hair out and tell Izzy where to put that giant patch of scalp.

Izzy was sabotaging himself and was scaring people off in droves. No wonder he hadn't had a meaningful relationship with a woman. Or a friend. Or for that matter anyone. Truth be told, he was just very annoying as he had an inability to monitor his behavior. In addition, he was unable to read social situations and get appropriate feedback from others much to his detriment. Izzy is at the other end of the spectrum when considering appropriate humor. The real basis for his behavior was rooted in a deep sense of insecurity and a need to be seen and heard. The insecurity then produced monumental amounts of anxiety which would then alienate him from others. When I think of Izzy, I think about the obnoxious third grade student in elementary school who raises his hand in response to every question. If not called on by the teacher, this child would yell out the answer for all to hear so that they could marvel at his incredible genius. Unfortunately, that child would then demean the other students in the class calling them slow and stupid. Kind of sounds like Izzy. Not a really good way to make friends and a guaranteed way to alienate others.

There are people out there who have it just right. They know when to be quiet, when to speak up and when to tell a good joke. These people fit in easily in any situation and their social skills are appropriate and easy. When I say easy, I mean that there is no stress and strain while fitting in. It's natural for them to easily find a way just as the converse is true. Some people try so hard that they self-defeat and get in their own way. If only there was a manual or daily advice from SIRI or ALEXA, we would all know what to do. What we should never do is to be someone other than our authentic self because the real you has a bad habit of eventually catching up to you anyway.

My recommendations are simple and very obvious. In no particular order they are;

- Tell a joke every day to someone. Not to your dog or cat.
- They'll laugh at anything to get a treat.
- Listen to something funny every day either on the radio, on Youtube or wherever you can find humor.
- Do something that's fun. Go find a zip-line or a toboggan or an ATV and do whatever you need to enjoy a new experience.
- Monitor your friends and minimize your time with those people who are toxic. Surround yourself with friends who tend to add as opposed to take away.
- Minimize your time reading newspapers and find movies that are positive.
- Go dancing, ride a bike, play bocce, rollerblade, drink wine, play cards, swim, sky dive, fly a kite, bake cookies, go out to eat, go to the beach, drink wine (I think I already said that but for, God's sake, do something.)

- Change. Not your socks or your underwear, but real change. Write up a lesson plan to increase your happiness and stop doing what you have done a million times before. You already know the result of that behavior.

12. APPLE STOCK... SOUNDS DUMB TO ME

Greg came to my office on a rainy Tuesday afternoon and proceeded to tell me that the rain reminds him of his life. When questioning him about this negative statement, he told me that he felt like the character in the Peanuts cartoon. He felt that he was always under what appeared to be a dust storm. In Greg's case, wherever he turned, he seemed to have bad luck in every area of his life. He was thirty-two at the time, single, with a relatively low level position despite a degree from a relatively prestigious university. He presented as a portly, appropriately dressed man with a lack of eye contact. Probably best to hear from Greg himself.

"Everything probably all started with the stories my Dad told me when I was growing up. He would tell me of what he called 'missed opportunities.' He had an opportunity to buy a significant amount of Polaroid stock when it was first offered to the public. Dad felt it was a trendy bad investment. But, later on, he came to realize that he could have retired had he invested in the stock. I heard the story over and over. But, that's not all. He had an opportunity to date the homecoming queen at his high school. But, he was too late in asking her out, like a year and a half late. Then there's the car he could have bought but he waited too long. By the time he was ready, the price rose above his price point. He could have bought a house at a real bargain price but, once again, he waited and waited until it was too late. He would use the word 'should' all the time to explain away his behaviors as if that word would make everything okay. It did not. After a while, I realized that he was a procrastinator and that decisions would reverberate in his head until he would lose out on countless opportunities. It seemed that his timing was always off causing him deep regrets. He used to joke about the fact that he had no luck and told me that if he ever won the lotto he knows he would be diagnosed with cancer within a week. Looking back on my dad's life, I see it was a life of regrets and poor timing. Not bad luck. I'm afraid that I am becoming my father.

A number of years ago I was offered an opportunity to buy a good deal of Apple stock and I remember saying to my broker that it sounded kind of dumb to me and it's probably just a fad. Every opportunity that presents itself to me I seem to screw up and I now have the same run of bad luck that my father had. I should have bought the stock. I should have applied for the new position in my firm. I should have asked Margaret from accounting to dinner instead of now watching that idiot Mel from sales take her out. I should have moved to the house that I looked at for months before someone else swooped in and underbid me. I should have taken the advancement course offered at work. Instead, now I answer to a woman who I trained when she began three years ago. I'm telling you my luck is terrible and it looks like it's never going to get much better."

After hearing his mournful tales of woe, we discussed the issues at hand which had nothing to do with luck. First, 'one should never should thyself.' Using this word means that you're replaying the negative past over and over. The word 'should' implies that something different could have been done at a different point in time. Didn't happen. Let it go.

Second, my belief is that you make your own luck. You don't wait for fate to intervene to brighten up your life. Many men and women complain about the difficulty in finding a significant other. Some people go to web sites to find dates. They also ask their friends if they know anyone suitable. They go to dances, single clubs, the library, the laundromat, a bocce tournament or any place where there is a possibility of making a connection. Some people go to work and then go home to complain about being lonely and not having someone. Do they expect that by chance the perfect individual will come to their door with glass slippers and ask them to go to the masked ball?

I also believe that you should always be looking for another job or promotion. I realize this not the norm but let's look at this a little more closely. Let's say that you have a great job with good co-workers and a good salary. You like it where you are, it's safe and you know the people and everything else about the company. Why wouldn't you look for a job that may offer more money, better chances for advancement, a better retirement plan, a closer commute etc.? You have nothing to lose if you look around while being secure in a job that you like. That's how you make your own luck. You advocate for yourself and you look to cut the best deal for yourself. Of course, there are many other factors that go into making a decision like this but you owe it to yourself to take care of yourself first.

Third, regarding decision making, you make a decision based upon gathering as much information possible at that time. Then, you evaluate your data and make a decision. Not information that you find out later, but information based upon what you know at the time when you actually make the decision. This could eliminate a number of "shoulds" when things do not go as well as planned.

Number four is what I call the game changer and it's been overused and misunderstood for years. This is the simple truth that timing is everything. Remember that really cute little thing you had a crush on in the third grade. You could have wooed her and taken her for an ice cream soda and then followed with a marriage proposal. Silly of course but what if the same spark was there and you met her again when you were both twenty-one. You'd need to lose the ice cream soda idea but you could substitute a good Merlot coupled with a kale salad and she would be yours until the next meal. A friend of mine first met his wife when he was twenty-nine and she was nineteen. They were both happily married and were taking courses at a local university. He was taking graduate courses while she was a sophomore studying biology. They met, they talked, they had coffee and they went their separate ways. Lo' and behold, they ran into each other at a softball game eleven years later and remembered their meeting at the university. As luck would have it they were both recently divorced and were ready to move on, and they did. No more sodas and they both hate kale now but the fact remains that the timing couldn't have been better for them.

The same way that you make your own luck, you can change the timing in your life. One of my patients, Roger, had a succession of what can only be described as horrific relation- ships during his adulthood. His first wife was, as he described her, the most controlling person in the fucking universe. He divorced her. The process of divorce lasted three years even though he had what he thought was an excellent attorney. It turns out that the attorney was an attractive woman looking for some changes in her life and Roger was to be that change. They married within a year when she dropped a bombshell and told him that she did not want to practice law any longer. So, she left her firm and dedicated herself to a career in wildlife photography. He became the sole breadwinner and supported her passion in every way. Down the line, he lost the home that he had purchased before he met her and then also ran into additional problems with the I.R.S. A divorce quickly followed sending him to another relation- ship with a woman who had money but chose not to spend it. She was holding on to her rubles, planning for an early retirement in the South Pacific. After a year, that relationship was over with even more financial difficulties lurking. Finally, he met an employed woman whom he found astoundingly beautiful and verbal. A match made in heaven. Or so it seemed. He found out that she had done prison time and was a convicted felon. He rationalized that it was all okay. It was a nonviolent crime because she only stole some money. That's all. To compound matters, as if this couldn't get any worse, she now ran a small movie company that produced XXX films. She denied ever being in the films themselves but there was a great deal of doubt regarding this. They broke up but Roger still talked to her on the phone and every year or so, they would get together at some mutually arranged place to have monumental sex. Roger always paid for the trip including the airfare, hotel and meals.

I'm happy to say that Roger then finally found his perfect mate. She was age appropriate and sexually active with a sharp bright wittiness about her. So far, so good although there were a few stumbling blocks stopping them from a bright chirpy future. It seemed that while he lived locally, she lived six hours away and would not be able to move for at least eight years. Not an overwhelming problem and not a real deal breaker. After all, he was wildly in love and love conquers all. The other stumbling block was the fact that she was married with three kids aged ten, thirteen and fifteen. The reason for the eight year wait was so that the youngest would be eighteen and he would be better able to deal with his parent's divorce. For more than three years Roger would leave work every other Friday and drive six hours to stay at a motel with the hopes that she could slip away for an hour or two. There were times when she was unable to meet him due to the kid's activities or other schedule conflicts but Roger persevered and made the trek at least twenty-six times a year.

Timing is everything and Roger had absolutely no sense of timing nor did he understand that his life was moving along while he was standing still. She finally broke up with Roger because she said that she felt too much pressure. Go figure.

You should be aware of the timing in your life. Where you are now? Where do you plan to be in a year, five years and so on? Do you have a time sensitive plan? Or are you stuck in quicksand and staying in the same place day after day? Roger's lack of timing was coupled with a secondary, much more debilitating disorder. There is no psychological diagnosis for this disorder although it is widespread and could be a life changer. In simple terms, Roger's 'pick' was broken. Yes, his 'pick' was irreparably broken and might be impossible to mend. 'Pick" refers to one's ability to pick the right person in a relationship. It refers to evaluating a person or a situation and being able to pick what is best. Then and only then, will you be able to determine if you need to run away from that person as if locusts were attacking.

The second truism which eludes many people can be seen in the cases of Charise and Selene. Charise was in her late forties and had worked as an assistant principal for a school system for thirteen years. Prior to the A.P. position, she taught a third grade class for eleven years. She was vested in a retirement program and would be able to retire in a few years. But, she expected to work another sixteen years to add to her pension. In her twenty-four years, she had taken on any and all additional assignments to increase her salary such as teaching hospital homebound, after school tutoring, teaching summer school and lunchroom supervision. She was married with no children. Her annual vacation consisted of going to the Jersey shore for a week staying in a small inexpensive inn. She and her husband had older cars and ate out once a week at a buffet. The problem arose when one considers her unrealistic goal which was to have more money than any of her co-workers and friends when she retired. A lofty and truly inappropriate goal for anyone as there will always be people retiring with more. What made this competition so outlandish was the fact that she would withhold all pleasure and enjoyment for the future possibility of having more money than her peers. This is akin to buying a thirty-two foot boat only to find that your friend just bought a thirty-seven foot boat. It is like bragging about your seven day Caribbean cruise only to find out that your friend just returned from a ten day cruise. The truism is that every- thing is relative. Yes, everything.

Selene was very similar to Charise except for the fact that Selene was already vested in a retirement system and could have retired five years ago. Rather than retire she continued to work and planned for the numerous trips she would take when she retired. She wanted more than her sister who married a doctor and was to retire very well in a home in Connecticut. Selene was a bit out of shape and decided that she would get healthy when she retired. Unfortunately, the powers to be had a different plan for her. That uncalled for plan was called cancer which curtailed both her career and her travel plans. She wanted more and lost herself in her constant quest to compete with her sister. Everything is relative. There are people with more and there are those with less. This is a nonnegotiable truth that stands up to the test of time. A friend of mine used to say that when you crave things that you don't have, you diminish what you do have. You should establish a true appreciation for what you have. You should develop a feeling of gratitude for what you have and an appreciation for everything positive in your life.

Finally, you should have an understanding of enough. You should answer the question, when is enough, enough. When will you have enough money to enjoy life and be happy? Do you really need that new car? Do you need the bigger boat? Do you have to keep accumulating money and pensions far in excess of what you truly need? This is a question that will be answered differently by everyone. The common denominator is whether or not your quest to accumulate and compete is interfering with your life. Are you really living? Or are you spinning your wheels until you realize that you've wasted a great deal of irreplaceable time?

13. I THINK I SEE A HAND
COMING OUT OF THE FLOOR

I t should be noted that I am regarded by my associates as warm, empathetic, and very understanding. I am also imbued with a set of characteristics that allow me to effectively practice the art of psychotherapy with one and all despite the lack of charm or attraction on the part of my patients. Despite years of vigorous training, I am still amazed at how quickly I can be thrown off track by a small number of my patients, such as Fran. Fran came to my office in late 2011 after a brief phone call to discuss my fees. Something about her manner of speaking put me on alert. She bounced between very rapid talk and long periods of silence. Not one to refuse a new patient, I decided that there were, in fact, bills to pay and that she really didn't seem to be all that bad.

Fran entered my office with a flourish as if the red carpet was before her and her entourage was soon to follow. Wearing a ratty mink coat in eighty degree weather was only one of twenty signs that were thrown out at me indicating that I should have run away as far as humanly possible. But I would not budge. She wore horn-rimmed glasses covered with rhinestones along with a coordinated mohair skirt, mohair sweater and a hat also made of the same material. As she sat, she smiled from ear to ear as if she had just told herself a terrific joke, or she was very flatulent. I was hoping it was a joke. Her demeanor, despite her smiling, was very aggressive as she challenged me on almost every question, even the basic information questions such as age and address. Fran was a thirty-seven year old Caucasian female and had moved into the area thirteen years ago after she married her husband. I would like to give the husband a name but Fran absolutely refused to give it to me. She told me that it was a secret. In retrospect, that was another sign that I should have heeded but did not. Fran was employed in a large office but she worked on computers in a small separate location away from her co-workers. I didn't understand that at the time but fully understand her separation now.

She told me that she had tried therapy three times in the past and not one of those overpaid morons knew a damn thing. Another sign held up for me to see, but alas I was blind. One last thing before we can discuss her difficulties. A few words about how she presented in as kind a manner as possible. She was by any measure unattractive. From her hair to her skin to her eyes to her stocky legs, she was someone people would distance themselves from by any means necessary, including jumping off a ship. Perhaps I'm being a little rude and uncaring but she was in need of a great deal of work. I imagine that what really exacerbated her unattractiveness was her persistent nastiness which she spewed out in abundance. Realizing that any question that I would pose to her would be met with anger, I asked her to just tell her story and then I would discuss what she said, and that's when the flood gates opened.

"At one point, I would have told you that I didn't know where to begin but since this is my fourth rodeo, I know just what you want. I hope you're more successful than the last three imbeciles I met with. They did nothing for me except to take my money and try to convince me that I'm in charge of my life. What absolute bullshit. Why do I need a therapist if I'm in charge and I need to do all the work? You guys are like frickin' weathermen who are almost always wrong but keep their jobs no matter how bad their forecasts are. Maybe they should just look out the window and report what they see. Maybe they'd get a forecast right. Morons. Where was I? Oh yeah. I need to begin.

I work in an office with more than fifty dull people. They have no sense of what a work ethic is. Nor do they understand how they should work with someone who is much brighter, namely me. After repeated clashes with these dolts, management moved me to a small private office so I wouldn't have to deal with them. One of these idiots actually told me that I was the cause of the discord and that's why I was moved. I gave her the finger and walked away as I have no time to deal with the likes of her. I work with numbers all day which is better than working with those people. I never go to lunch with any of them and I take my breaks alone eating carrots, my favorite food.

I don't know if you believe in coincidences but my current job is very much like my last three jobs. Different people with the same low IQs in positions that were way over their heads. First, they disagree with me. Then, management gets involved and I'm moved to a new, more isolated part of the office. Why should I be moved for God's sake? They're the losers. Do they have some kind of manual that tells them to move the bright one's away from the herd? It's ridiculous and it needs to be stopped. My husband and I have sued all three companies for their unfair treatment and we have spent a great deal of money trying to rectify this abuse. Two of the cases were lost but we're hoping that the third one will be a winner. I should also mention to you that I have filed suit against all three of my therapists due to their incompetence. I reported two of them to the American Psychiatric Association and the other one I picketed outside of his office for two full weeks. I can't do that anymore due to a shmucky restraining order so I guess I'll have to sue him also. If I were you, I'd make sure that you do a much better job than they did."

At that point, I wrote a reminder to make sure to increase my malpractice coverage. I also began to make a plan to terminate Fran as soon as humanly possible. I gathered my strength, leaned back and continued to listen, but she stopped talking and just stared into space for the longest minute of my life. I had no idea if she was formulating her thoughts, having petite mal seizures or was lost in her own maze of thinking. Finally, she looked at me and continued.

"As a child, I was raised by my aunt and uncle who

told me that my parents died in a car accident in the Azores while on holiday. I never believed that story but they never budged from the original Azores story. Where the hell are the Azores anyways? My aunt and uncle were very reclusive and never went out unless necessary. They didn't have children of their own so I became their only child. I always did well in school but most of the kids were just plain dumb and couldn't relate to me. The same thing in high school where I was happiest being by myself and away from all the other stupidity. College was basically the same with the exception of the fact that I met my husband in our senior year. We dated for three years and then decided to get married and go to the Poconos. He works for a company that translates books into Esperanto and, sometimes, does some Arabic translations. He's a good man. Not as bright as me. But he tries. The major problem is his E.D. You must know what that is. At least, I hope you do. He cannot maintain an erection for more than twenty or thirty seconds and it takes me much, much longer than that. Thank God I met Johnny."

Once again, she wandered into her own Neverland and left me sitting and praying that when she returned to earth, it would not be with graphic erotic stories of Johnny. I looked at my watch and found that the second hand appeared to be moving in slow motion and that this session was feeling like root canal. Once again, I relaxed and waited for what was to come, hoping not to bring my lunch up.

"I was leaving the office on the way to my car when I saw Johnny for the first time. I realized that I had seen him in the building from a distance but I never realized just how incredibly sexy he was. I decided right there and then that I would be going to bed with him even though I didn't know his name at that time. I went into spy mode and, after a few days, found the firm he worked for and saw his name on his office door. From there it was easy. All you have to do is hire a P.I. and they can get all the information that you need. I found out that he had worked at that firm for three years and lived a half hour away with a wife and two kids. Now, I knew what to do. Before you even judge me, I'll tell you that I have no qualms about pursuing a married man. If he had any scruples, he simply had to say no and the deal is done. If he had a problem keeping his penis in his pants, it's his problem and certainly not mine. I began to accidentally bump into him, sometimes three times in a day, until he began to really notice me. I'll spare you all the lurid details but let's say that, eventually, he went a lot longer than twenty or thirty seconds. We would both take what we called 'motel days' and we would both call in sick at work. We stayed in the same Howard Johnson and we didn't just sample the flavors of ice cream. He was remarkable in every way and I decided that I wanted more. After all, there are Howard Johnson's all over the United States and I wanted to travel. I began to plan a future with Johnny. One with a good deal of sex and a great deal of travel. I was happier then than I had been for a long, long time. Then, he dumped me. Can you believe it? He dumped me like a piece of yesterday's trash that you set out at the curb. He told me that it was his problem alone and not my problem. As if I didn't already know that. He told me that he wasn't good enough for me, I knew that also. But what really pissed me off is that he told me that he still loved his wife and wanted to try to have a better marriage. Was he so damn blind that he couldn't see that he already had the best he would ever get? Why the fuck do you look for something else when you already have me?

I wrote him letters and he didn't respond. Then I started to text him every day. Sometimes, ten times in a day. No response. I sent flowers to his office and to his home and didn't get a response. I followed him to his home after work one day and he told me to leave him alone or he'd see an attorney. I contacted him on Facebook, Twitter, YouTube and any other site to get him to respond but he wouldn't even give me the courtesy of a response. The P.I. that I hired kept following him for two more weeks until Johnny confronted him and told him to stop. It was right after that I received my first restraining order. But, not my last. So, last week, I went to an artist friend of mine and asked him to design a calendar with pictures of Johnny and I in different positions, if you know what I mean? I only have one picture of the two of us but my friend said it would be easy to make up the pictures based upon the photo. It should be ready next week and I can't wait to mail Johnny the first edition. I'll probably sign the inside cover. After all it is a first edition and probably will be worth a shitload of money someday."

It was time for me to take a break and to try to get some clarity and figure out what was going on. Her pathology was rampant on a number of levels and I needed time to sort things out. I asked her questions about her marriage, her position at work, her hobbies and anything else I could think of to get a more cogent picture of her personality. In the next session, yes there was a next session, I asked for a chronology of the events in her affair with Johnny.

"I moved here with my husband, Voldemort, thirteen years ago and began a new job almost immediately. I met Johnny twelve years and eight months ago on that fateful day. He broke up with me twelve years and seven months ago after the best sex anyone has ever had. I will never give up my Johnny because I know what true love is and I know that Johnny would be better off with me than his dull, drab asshole wife. I really don't know what else you want from me. I've given you all the information that you need. All I need is Johnny."

I sat there for a two full minutes unable to believe that the affair was twelve and a half years ago and she was acting as if it happened last week. Her life was consumed by an affair that had ended so long ago it should have been old, old news. The level of angst in discussing her issue was completely and absolutely out of proportion to the time element involved. While I sat there in utter silence for those two minutes, I realized that, once again, Fran had drifted into her land beyond. I called out to her and she looked at me and said those eleven words that would clarify everything. She said, "I think I see a hand coming out of the floor."

What the hell was that all about? She kept staring at the floor and didn't move a muscle as if she were in a deep trance. As a trained professional, I knew not to confront her hallucination as that could be dangerous to me. So, we both stared for ten full minutes. She stared at the imaginary hand while I stared at her psychotic break and hoped to make a clean getaway from the office without a major incident.

The second session was the last session that I had with Fran as her pathology did not lend itself to therapy. There would be no insight and no great changes in her behavior seeing a therapist once or twice a week. Fran needed medication and possibly placement in a treatment center. She was experiencing two of the hallmark symptoms for a psychosis, delusions and hallucinations. A delusion is a false persistent belief maintained in spite of evidence to the contrary. Fran was exhibiting delusions of grandeur and an inappropriate sense of self. The hand coming out of the floor was indicative of a hallucination where an individual sees or hears things that are not really there. Put this altogether and you have a diagnosis of a psychosis, a major mental disorder where contact with reality is impaired.

Reality is the true key to understanding Fran and many others although most individuals will likely present with a lesser degree of pathology. Reality refers to the quality of being real. It is authentic, objective and true to life and it cannot be changed. It refers to the ability to see life as it is and not how you would like it to be. It includes accurate self-perception, accurate perception of your environment and true perception of others. Our reality is constantly being questioned and we all learn through a process called reality testing how to separate what is real from what is not real.

Imagine walking home from the movies with your friend after seeing a movie about space monsters. Out of the corner of your eye, you see movement by a bush next to the sidewalk. Your friend screams and runs away telling you that the monsters have arrived and that they want to kill you. As she runs away, you look a little closer and see that it's a cat. Your friend's reality testing stopped working for a few moments in this instance. If this behavior is a part of her everyday life then there is the potential for a huge problem. If this is a rarity then it could be nothing more than a brain-fart and all is well. We do our own reality checks all the time, every single day. You wake up in the morning with a red mark on your arm and by the end of the day you have convinced yourself that you have skin cancer. You awake with a stomach ache and you suspect abdominal cancer. Your friend doesn't call you for a day and you're frantic to find out why he hates you so suddenly. All of the above can be explained away by taking one's time and analyzing the total situation. That red mark on your arm is a mosquito bite. Your stomach upset is the result of a bad garbanzo bean. Finally, your friend who has become hateful lost his cell phone. You can't change reality no matter how hard you try. Suffering the consequences of a breakup, as in Fran's case, is very difficult but no matter how long you grieve and stay angry the fact remains that it's over and all that's left is for you to get over it and move on. Very easy to say but very difficult to do. Sometimes, we like to live in our pain a little too long.

I had a patient a number of years ago who came to me just before she was going to court for sentencing by a judge. She was a bright active woman of twenty-five with no criminal history. It appears that she had accumulated a total of seven traffic tickets ranging from illegal parking to speeding. In addition, she had just been arrested for her third DUI in four years. Everything finally caught up to her and she was scheduled to have her day in court. I suspected that she would not be home for dinner that evening. I asked her why she didn't pay for the tickets or show up for her court dates. She offered what she thought was a logical explanation. When she received a ticket, citation or an order to appear, she would put them in the glove box of her car. In her world, once they were out of sight and put away, they ceased to exist. Seven tickets and two court orders to appear in court magically disappeared forever by simply putting them in a glove box. What was most surprising was that this was done by a very bright, affable young woman who seemed to be very much in touch with reality. The defense mechanism called denial has been stated to be the most primitive of all the defense mechanisms. Denial is the simple refusal to accept and face what is real. This young lady cornered the market on denial and I understand that the same inability to see and deal with reality led to her serving six years in prison for a number of other offenses, including theft. Not a happy ending.

In the long run, Fran, of mink coat fame, was involuntarily committed to an institution where she was placed in charge of the daily calendars of the other patients. I have a framed and signed copy of her first Johnny edition calendar. It's worth a shitload of money now.

14. WHY DID MY DOG HAVE TO DIE, HE WAS ONLY NINETEEN?

C hange is inevitable. How profound is that? I really don't believe that too many people are surprised by this fact. What is surprising is how incapable most of us are when confronted by changes. One of my patients, a man of sixty-five lost his wife more than twenty years prior and not a day went by where he didn't grieve her death. I fully understand the incredible pain one experiences when you lose a mate, especially a partner of twenty-seven years, but life moves on. This particular patient was afraid to move on and was unable to cope with the changes in his life.

In contrast, I present the opposite point of view. In case A we have a woman married to a man for more than thirty years. They had three grown children and, by all accounts, they had a loving, caring marriage. Her husband became very ill and died after about three years from the onset of his illness. A month after his funeral, she began to go on dating sites looking for a man. She started dating in earnest six weeks after the funeral and was married in less than a year. Her explanation was that you only live once and grieving accomplishes nothing. She further felt that her husband would have wanted her to be happy and why should she deny herself. Some people might regard this as callous and unfeeling but in her mind it was the rational and appropriate thing to do. I should mention that all three of her children did not agree with her choice. It led to a good deal of turmoil and discord which lasted years.

Case B is similar in many ways except for the shorter time frame. In this case, we have a happily married couple with two children under five. Suddenly, the wife became extremely ill with a deadly case of leukemia passing after only three days in the hospital. He openly told everyone at the funeral that he couldn't live without her. He also told everyone that he had to have a woman in his life or he couldn't survive. To cut to the chase, he married again two months after his wife's death. He was an apparently bright, normal man who was totally unable to deal with a profound change in his life. He also had the remarkable capacity to remove her from his memory and would not permit any discussion about her and her untimely death. If friends or relatives would bring her up, he would get angry and tell them to stop bringing up old news.

What you have here is profound change and the inability to deal with its ramifications. Let's look at another example. You wake up one morning and decide that you want a pet. Doesn't make any difference what you are looking for. It could be a dog, a cat, a hamster, a manatee or a miniature pig. The good news is that you'll love them to death and the bad news is that, at some point, they will die. You know that when you get them as you are opening yourself up for some future heartbreak. To make matters worse, human are the only animals with the knowledge that they will die at some point. Pets just go merrily on their way bringing us joy while we worry constantly about their health because we know how their story is going to end. One of my patients actually questioned why her nineteen year old dog had to die. Change can be a real bummer.

Change has been defined as substituting or replacing something with something else. Another equally confusing way of looking at change is when you put or take something in place of something else. What's important to note is the fact that you lose the original item when you change. Some individuals are unable to cope with any loss causing change to become tortuous on any and all levels.

If you've ever moved from one neighborhood to another or from one city to another, I invite you to go back for a visit. Walk around your old neighborhood and see all the changes since you left. Does it look as nice? Usually, it doesn't quite look as you remembered it. Most people don't like the changes. If you get a chance go back to your old elementary school and see all the changes. Has it changed? Of course it has,. Everything has. Many people find it remarkable to go back to a place and see all the changes that have taken place. Some people just accept the fact that change is constant and inevitable.

Food tastes different also. Remember the great pizza you had at the local restaurant when you were a child? If you tasted it again, you would find that, in many cases, the food is just not the same. If you really want to rattle your memory bank go to a high school or college reunion. Everyone, including yourself has changed and many times not for the better. We try to recapture our looks by dieting before a reunion. We try a new hairstyle and have our legs waxed while picking up a killer dress or suit. Change is the only constant in a world where everything is changing.

A former patient of mine in his late forties ran into his ex- wife at a restaurant in his home town. He told me that he didn't recognize her. In fact, he was about to hit on her when she came over to greet him. New five inch heels along with a thirty five pound weight loss turned her into a different woman. She also was smartly dressed and carried herself with a great deal of confidence. She had changed dramatically in a number of years. My patient was so in awe of the difference that he embarked on a program to re-do himself. He went to the gym, stopped smoking and lost forty pounds. It seems that the ex was a terrific catalyst for him to change.

Do things really change? Or do we tend to live our lives in a similar fashion every day? As you get older people tend to live life in a comfortable rhythm like playing a familiar song on the piano over and over. We become more and more comfortable with our life patterns and are thrown off track when confronted with change. We live, in many instances, in a rut which is defined as a grave that is open on both ends. We tend to feel more comfortable in our own little ruts and have a good deal of anxiety when taken out of our comfort zone. Look at your daily life and try to see how predictable it is.

Think about the following and ask yourself if you're in a rut.

- Do you set an alarm every night? If so, is it set to the same time?
- Do you sleep on the same side of the bed every night?
- Do you read a book or the same anything every night?
- Do you sleep on your back or your right side or your left side?
- Do you fluff your pillow every night? Do you turn it over every night to get to the cool side?
- Do you sleep with some light on such as a night light?
- Do you wear something similar to sleep every night even though you wouldn't be caught dead wearing it in front of friends?
- Assuming you get a good night's rest do you wake up at the same time?
- Once awake, what do you do? Many people have a very well established routine for the morning which includes brushing their teeth, urinating, defecating, hand washing, face scrubbing, flossing and a multitude of other behaviors usually done in the same order, every day. Every single day.
- Once up do you wear another outfit? Or do you simply cover your ratty night clothes with an equally unattractive robe?

- Do you sit at the same place at the same table to eat every morning?
- Do you drink the same thing every day?
- Do you eat basically the same thing almost every morning?
- Do you read a newspaper every morning and the go on to complain about the state of the world?
- Do you watch television and the same newscasters every day?

You get where I'm going with this. Most people live a programmed life with little variation whatsoever. For some people, there is comfort in routine. Unfortunately, there is also boredom and joy is not to be found. I taught a class at a university a few years ago on happiness. The class consisted primarily of adults from fifty to seventy. One of my assignments was to have them sleep on the other side of the bed for three nights. I realized that most of the people were in a relationship and that they had to get consent from the other person to do this. They all agreed to try this even though a good number of them thought that it was so easy, it was kind of silly.

A week later, when I entered the class my students were animated and bustling about discussing the experiment. Out of twenty-seven students, only four, yes four, were able to do the whole three nights. Six were able to do one night and four were able to do two nights. The remaining thirteen students could not complete even one night of discomfort. It was remarkable how easily they were thrown out of their nice customary zone and into the discomfort zone. I wanted to suggest that they try a few more tasks such as changing their bathing time from morning to night and vice versa but I believed that task would have sent a number of them over the edge. I gave them all an A and a big smiley face.

There's nothing wrong with routine. We all have routines and we're the better for it. To live randomly is to live as a schizophrenic. However, one needs to look at your own degree of routine to see if your life has lost a bit of its luster. What is interesting is the fact that everything around us is in a state of flux and some of us try to remain exactly the same. Everything is cyclical and ever changing. We tend to robotically do the same thing day after day.

Some individuals have a much more difficult time dealing with change than others. There are three significant areas that pose monumental problems for people when it comes to change. There are those of us trying to hold on to our youthful looks. Another group includes those individuals who are losing skills due to age such as athletes. Finally, the third group consists of people transitioning from work to retirement. I mention these three groups only to give you a representative sample of situations as the list is obviously open to amendment.

We are, as a country, obsessed with our looks and the maintenance of a youthful appearance. We really don't like to age because really weird things happen and we don't like some of the changes. What's the deal with the hair growing on my back, or on my chin? What's the deal with these dark spots on my hands? What's with the bags under my eyes? I already have luggage. There's more and more hair on my pillow when I wake. Since when do I need three pairs of glasses? Why does my belly stick out further than my breasts? Cellulite? No frickin' way. This can go on forever. As someone once said, "Getting old is not for the faint of heart."

We would all like to keep our looks and avoid the numerous and unavoidable signs of aging. However, if you read closely I used the word 'unavoidable' when discussing the signs of aging. Both men and women fight the effects with varying degrees of success. We try Botox, sculpting, surgery, yoga, face creams and gels and KFC extra crispy all to no avail. Perhaps I shouldn't include KFC as I believe that I may be the only person in the western hemisphere who can rationalize a crispy chicken breast as a youth enhancer. Are you ready for the bad news? The best you can do is to accept the fact that you will age and attempt to age gracefully. We never get any younger but we are always getting older. Sorry, but reality can be a real bummer at times. So, lose those shorty-shorts and the new tattoos at the age of sixty-five. Throw away the five inch heels and just calm down and stop fighting, you'll be a lot happier.

Athletes can have a very difficult time with change and the aging process. The quarterback has lost a bit of his speed and his arm tires easier. The tennis player cannot get around the court fast enough. The everyday jogger doesn't seem to be able to run as fast or as long as she once could. Surprise, surprise, surprise! Why are some people so unprepared for the inevitable? Why can't they accept the simple fact that we all age and with that revelation is the need to accept the changes that come with aging?

The third group constitutes an enormous number of people as this group includes all those people who are retiring, retired, or considering retirement in their future. This is a very difficult transition. In many cases you lose your identity which had been defined by your work prior to retirement. This change is monumental as it constitutes a new lifestyle, new friends, new locations and a number of other factors. I was discussing retirement with a friend of mine a number of years ago. He had retired a few years before at the ripe old age of fifty-two. He told me something very important that I didn't really understand at that time. He told me that people need what he called 'retirement skills'.

He said that you need to have a definite plan which should include what you will do every day. He said that a day without work and with nothing planned stretches out forever. He further stated that many people who don't plan wind up going back to work out of sheer boredom. Another friend of mine told me that he was going to retire and I mentioned the concept of retirement skills. He told me that his plan was to catch up on all the reading he had missed in the past thirty years. He had a list of one hundred books and he was going to read them in order from cover to cover. Even though he was a slow reader, he went back to work after six months. Retirement is tricky, the day is long and you can't be busy all the time. So sharpen up those skills cause big changes are a comin'.

What can you do to change your life a wee bit and put some excitement back in your otherwise predictable routine? It would be impossible to list all the possible changes that you can make as our life circumstance are all unique, but look through the random list that follows and consider attempting a few of the suggestions. They are, in no particular order as follows: change sides of the bed; change your alarm time; change your cereal; change your eggs; buy different coffee; eat at another location; eat a different kind of ethnic food; change where you sit at home to eat; change where you sit to read; try a different route to work; ride a bicycle; ride a unicycle; go on a diet; call your ex; decide to gain weight; workout; travel; go to a zoo; call a friend; arrange a party; ride a camel; watch different television stations; go to a concert; listen to

A.M. radio; talk to Alexa; drive someplace without your GPS; go a day without your phone; go a month without your phone; don't text for a day; unfriend everyone on Facebook; buy flowers ; read a different newspaper; eat at KFC; make yourself a root beer float; eat onion dip; set up a blog; buy yourself a gift; tell a joke; go dancing; go zip-lining; go water skiing; buy someone else a gift; buy me a gift; wash your car; re-wash it because you missed some spots; travel; make plans to travel; call brothers or sisters; call parents; and so on. The list is never ending and only you know what needs to change. I wish you well on your voyage of discovery.

15. DO I LOOK FAT?

There are few questions that bring about more fear than the simple inquiry, "Do I look fat?" Once these simple four words are spoken you will need cunning and stealth to disentangle yourself from an answer that could lead to monumental discord. Many people have been able to extricate themselves from this horrendous situation unscathed. Unfortunately many people fail miserably. The drama involved relates to the ego and it touches a raw nerve in everyone. The ego is the part of our personality that deals with the external world. It is the mediator between the id and the superego and represents how we see ourselves in the real world. In addition we all have what is termed an ego ideal which is a conception of ourselves as a better or more successful self. Sometimes the ego ideal begins to actually take over the ego and we are left with an individual who constantly strives to have himself or herself appear better than they are. These are those individuals who have to let you know all about their wonderfulness even though you never asked. I have three personal instances that will illustrate this pathology and they have all been observed by me firsthand, and these are not patients.

In the first case my wife and I were traveling on a beach vacation some years ago. We became friendly with a small group of fellow travelers with common interests. One couple, in their mid-thirties appeared to always have the best bathing suits, the best snorkel gear, wonderful bling jewelry, and everything else. This in itself was unremarkable but what was remarkable was the fact that they had to tell everyone exactly what everything cost. His bathing suit cost $160 and hers was

$250. Their snorkels were $110 each and they were made in France. They wore matching Mercedes baseball hats and Piaget watches at $6,000 each. That night at dinner he told us that his shirt was made by Kiton at a cost of $545 and she told us three times that her pants cost $300. Their list of items purchased was endless as was their conversation which bordered on obnoxious. In reality it didn't border, it crossed the line into the realm of the fully obnoxious.

Most people began to distance themselves from this unfortunate couple but I found it intriguing that two apparently normal people could be so out of touch with the effect they had on others. What was really of interest to me was how they could sneak a topic into a conversation in order to be able to tell everyone more about themselves. On our second night with the group I saw them work their magic. While eating dinner the husband suddenly jumped up from the table and ran to the edge of the dining room pointing up at the ceiling. We all looked at his little sprint wondering what the hell was going on. Was there an eagle stuck in the rafters? Was there a hole in the roof and we were in imminent danger of a total collapse? We all waited for him to come back to explain what had just happened. Of course some naïve soul at the table asked what was going on and fell right into his devious trap. He told everyone at the table that he's an architectural engineer and was looking at the trusses holding up the roof. Then he launched into a history of trusses followed by the complete chronology of his under-graduate schooling and the graduate schools he attended. This was followed by a list of his impeccable credentials. You could actually see everyone at the table lapse into a coma and take a step back by the time he finished his acceptance speech. Did anyone ask him what he did for a living? Did anyone ask him what his shirt cost? Did anyone really give a damn? The answer to all three questions is an emphatic 'no'. This is a couple with a weak ego and a need to elevate themselves over others to feed their ego. I did kind of like the shirt though.

The second example took place, once again, on vacation. We were fortunate enough to stay at a small castle in Scotland called Bruloch Castle. One night after dinner we went for an after dinner drink at the small, intimate bar that sat no more than ten people. We were having a grand time talking about what we had done that day and our plans for the next day. We tend to laugh a good deal more than most people and we were noticed by a couple a few stools away. The man had a terrible cough and the woman appeared to be totally disinterested in him. Finally out of the blue she left him and he approached us remarking that it appeared that we were having a good time. No problem at this point as he introduced himself as Barry Bruloch. How's that for coincidence, Barry Bruloch in Bruloch Castle in the wilds of Scotland. That's when the proverbial turd hit the fan as I fell into the trap and asked him if he's related in any way to the castle family. One simple, exceedingly dumb question on my part brought forth a half hour of non-stop commentary by Barry. See how easy it is to fall into their cleverly laid traps

Barry was in his early sixties and carried an extra fifty or sixty pounds on his medium frame. Well dressed with a very expensive but well-worn suit he had a jowly appearance and reminded me of Alfred Hitchcock. Coughing from the bottom of his lungs, the first thing he told us was the fact that his cough was not contagious, which still did not make me happy to have him three feet from us. With that cough disclaimer he proceeded to talk about himself and who he was and who he is and on and on. I will list what I learned about Barry during that lost half hour.

- He was distantly related to the Bruloch Castle family and came to see what the relationship was, there was none.
- He retired as a physician a few years ago after practicing more than thirty years.
- He went to Princeton on an academic scholarship and was third in his class.
- He has a home in San Francisco worth two million and a home in New York worth a million and a half.

- He practiced medicine in Chicago and had one of the largest practices in the city.
- He loves cars and has at different times in his life owned a Ferrari and two Maserati's
- He owned two restaurants in New York at one point and sold them both at a huge profit.
- He had season tickets to all the professional sports teams in both San Francisco and New York in case there was a game he wanted to see.
- We heard a very long explanation of the difficulty of obtaining malpractice insurance and the enormous expense involved.
- There was another long conversation about what a great investor he was and that he has made bundles from the stock market.
- We heard about his college football career when he was a starter at Princeton.
- We heard about his four grandkids. We heard that they are so bright that the schools just can't give them work to do on a high enough level.

He droned on and on in between coughing bouts causing my wife and I to glaze over despite the fact that he was in very close proximity. What is most interesting about this entire exchange is the simple fact that there was no exchange. After introducing himself we lost our chance to speak as Barry obviously needed to be heard. Once during a particularly bad coughing episode I was able to say "wow". One simple "wow" and he then took the floor and spoke endlessly. My question is very simple.

What do I know about Barry and what does he know about me? The answer is easy, I know much too much about him and he knows absolutely nothing about me.

After being verbally barraged by Barry we understood why his wife left and went to bed. We also understood that we both could not take another half an hour of Barry-boy so I used a technique that I had used just once before. I'm not proud of this technique but it always works and my mental health is more valuable to me than Barry's ego. When Barry finally realized that it would be a good idea to hear me talk, he asked me what kind of work I did. So I lied. I told him that my wife and I started a dot-com eight years ago and we sold it two years ago for thirty million dollars. I then told him that we travel between our three homes in Paris, Boston and Grand Cayman. What a remarkable quieting effect this had and still has. We have been tempted to use what we call "The Bruloch Technique" a number of times since the encounter with Barry but have fought off the urge.

Barry intrigued me to a point where we were forced to whip out a lie, which I felt was totally justified. I like to protect myself and my wife. Barry and the couple from the beach vacation were abusing the defense mechanism of identification. In both these instances they had a need to be more than they were. They identified with someone or something of illustrious value to increase their self-worth. I wish them all well and I hope that the architect finds his trusses and that the doctor finds a good pulmonologist.

As luck would have it my third encounter happened just a week ago right in my home town of Holmes Beach, Florida. Holmes Beach is located on a beautiful barrier island with an eight mile stretch of white sand. There are over sixty restaurants in three separate small towns on the island. It is a truly wonderful place to live with a relatively mixed population of tourists and locals. The island life-style is reminiscent of what many people call "Old Florida" in many ways with a relaxed pace and where many of the locals can be found at their favorite watering holes on a regular basis.

It was at one of these relaxed friendly places that my wife and I encountered our latest person of intrigue. We were watching a football game at a sports bar two miles from our house and minding our business. Our favorite team was ahead by twelve but the toughest part of the game was to come from the man sitting next to me. He was about forty with funky new age red sunglasses wearing a Tommy Bahama shirt. Short and very thin he had a full mustache and not a single hair on his head. His name was Manny. Our meeting went as follows to the best of my recollection as he started with a simple inane question.

"So where are you folks from?" "We live here on the island." "What town on the island?" "Holmes Beach."

"Where in Holmes Beach?"

"Let's just say the middle of Holmes Beach. Why do you ask?"

"The reason I ask is that we used to live in Holmes Beach but we decide to upscale and moved to Longboat Key about a year ago."

"We're very happy for you," I said with a wee bit of sarcasm as by telling me that he left to upscale he also attempted to diminish where I live. I knew there was probably a great deal more of this coming but I couldn't imagine the sheer volume of bragging that was in our future. Taking a sip from his beer he turned to us and began his litany of life.

"I really liked it in Holmes Beach but when you have three homes (another chance meeting with someone with multiple homes) you need good people to take care of things for you when you're not around. We need our Longboat house to be near the yacht we've been building for three years now. Started just a drop over three years now and it should be ready to go in about six months at a minimum. We're going to yacht (note that he'll "yacht" not sail and not cruise) from here to our other homes in Miami and Lake Michigan and we'll move with the seasons. I'm used to this kind of life because I ran the General Motors submarine division for more than twenty years. That was a great gig. I'd go from coast to coast every other week. There's great money in submarines if you have the right gig. Finding the right job is just a matter of being in the right place at the right time and knowing the right people. You also need talent, a great deal of talent if you want to be successful. When I was in my early thirties I was playing the guitar and singing my own songs at my own gigs. I play four instruments and I've been able to more than hold my own with other professionals. Every time someone would approach me with a proposition to join a band I would turn them down and I'll tell you why. I turned them down because they all wanted me to play with really bad musicians and I wouldn't have that. One night three guys came up to me and talked to me about starting a band. Actually they already had a band and wanted to know if I wanted to join them. Their band had some local success and they needed another guitarist, a second guitarist, not a lead guitar. I went and listened to them and they were nowhere near as good as I was so I told them to take a walk. Never saw them again. I still play gigs at one of the local bars two nights a week and I've been doing it for ten years. I probably could have been a star in the music business but there are too many idiotic untalented people trying to rip you off.

Like I said it's all about knowing all the right people. I know all the important people on the island. It's a way to get ahead because they all respect you for who you are. They all know me and I could probably be mayor on Longboat if I wanted it. Politics are no big deal, just a poor paying gig."

This kind of verbiage went on for what seemed like hours although in real time it was no more than twenty minutes. Twenty minutes of pure unadulterated hell we were forced to endure at our favorite watering hole. There was more, much more, and it was all the same egocentric dribble. Was I tempted to tell him what to do with all his gigs, of course I was. Did I want to challenge him on a number of other issues, absolutely! My wife, a much kinder and better person than I, whispered for me to be kind as she felt sorry for him.

Do you know that feeling you get when someone speeds by you doing a hundred and twenty on a highway and you pray for the police to be around? Do you also know the feeling that you get when you see the speeder pass an unmarked police car which then sets off his six light bars and chases the speeder? Feels kind of good and karmic, the universe is in tune, the right time and the right place. Manny came crashing down to the ground the same way the speeder did and it was a sight to behold.

At one point during the recitation of his wonderfulness someone in close proximity was admiring a painting that was for sale hanging right behind the bar. There were about six or seven large paintings on sale and they were in fact both tropical and very beautiful. The sale prices ranged from six hundred to well over two thousand dollars. Manny leaned over to me and told me that his wife was the artist and in fact all of the paintings displayed that day were his wife's. My wife, who loves art, then leaned over and told him that he should be very proud of his wife's work. Manny thanked my wife for the compliment and assured us that he would mention her kind comments to his wife when he gets home. Remember that timing is everything and in this case timing was the undoing of Manny. Ten minutes later guess who should come waltzing into our little bar? Why it was Manny's wife, the artist. Both my wife and I wanted to discuss her art and tell her how much we admired her work. As we got up to talk to her Manny appeared to be upset and in some sort of inner turmoil. He asked us what we're doing and we told him we were going to talk to his wife about her work. He then told us that he never said she was the artist. He was adamant and totally denied telling us what we both heard. He said that he knows the artist but denied telling us that his wife was the painter despite telling both of us twice. Busted. This is the feeling you get when the unmarked car chases the speeder. This is when any and all credibility that Manny once held was gone, and gone forever. Pitiful. We decided to just pay our bill and leave. No words were needed at that time, or would be needed ever. We plan on sitting in the front row at his next gig.

So how does this help you? There are a number of things to keep in mind. First, when you meet people are they more interested in themselves than they are in you? If they are self absorbed you need to proceed with caution and probably walk away. Second, you need to self-examine to make sure that you're not a Manny, a Barry Bruloch or a trusser. If you think you are, knock it off, it's not an endearing quality. If you know someone like one of these three people try to tell them with kindness and compassion that what they're doing is not in their best interest. Finally, are you fat? Only you really can answer that question and it's really only important for you and no one else. Your ego is your ego and you need to protect this entity to the fullest extent possible. You just never want to be Bruloched!

16. SHE'S EVERYTHING I'VE EVER LOOKED FOR IN A WOMAN EXCEPT FOR THAT ONE LITTLE ANNOYING THING

Relationships can best be described as complex, intricate, confusing, difficult, perplexing and muddled to say the least. There are so many variables involved in a relationship between two people that the possible combinations of traits and characteristics can run into the millions. The first task that we are saddled with is to find the right person. But before you can do that you need to ask yourself what a good relationship is. It would be virtually impossible to find that wonderful compadre if you're not sure what you're looking for. How will you know if you've found that diamond and avoided all the false gold?

To begin, you need to make a list that includes what you believe are the attributes of a good relationship from your personal point of view. Depending on a number of factors (age, religion, socio-economic, location, etc.), your list could include anywhere from five to fifty attributes. There are no correct or incorrect answers so go get a pen and paper and be honest with what you believe a good relationship entails. If you are currently in a relationship, make your list and then see how your real life relationship measures up to your concept of the ideal relationship. The closer the two are the better. But, if you find a great disparity between the two then you have some work in front of you.

Save your pen and paper and make another list including ten characteristics of the person you are seeking as an ideal soulmate. If you are already in a relationship, you need to hide this list from your significant other and be honest with yourself. Once again, the more in sync the list is with your actual partner, the better the prognosis. Unfortunately, if the lists are very much in disagreement, you need to prepare yourself for a little more work. If you peruse the internet, you will find thousands of pages written concerning what men want and what women want in a mate. I've taken the liberty of reviewing many lists and came up with lists that are representative of what we want in a mate (according to the always correct internet).

Beginning with what women want, here are the ten most desirable characteristics in reverse order starting with number ten. They are as follows;

- Passionate and adventurous
- Intelligent
- Patient
- Dependable
- Shared values

- Thoughtful and generous
- Empathetic
- Confident about his appearance
- A good listener
- Humorous (Did I tell you the joke about the rabbi and the nun?)

There it is in a nutshell. But let's look at what women definitely do not want. In no particular order:

- Unreliability
- Poor work ethic
- Selfishness
- Men who send mixed signals
- Men who don't take care of themselves
- Also other factors such as cheapness, jealousy, too dominant, too submissive, too wild, too tame, too well endowed, not at all endowed and a slew of others.

So, now you have a vague idea of what women both want and don't want. Let's stop for a moment and look at what men want and don't want. Once again in reverse order the eight things men want are:

- A woman with a great vibe
- A woman to have great sex with
- A compatible woman
- Someone with dreams and goals for herself

- Someone to share his dreams and goals
- A good listener
- A woman to share his passion
- A need to be attracted to that person

THAT'S IT, directly from the infallible internet. Now, you are so well informed that you can mold yourself into that person that men want. Not so easy. Now a short list of what men don't want, not in any particular order. They do not want;

- Power struggles
- Cheating
- Drama
- Women who want too much
- Moodiness
- Her not saying what she means
- Boring sex

There you have it. You should be well versed on what the other sex wants and doesn't want. Everything you have just read, all four lists, are rubbish. Yes, I made you read all this rubbish because you can't work off a list when there are so many intangibles to consider. I apologize for being slightly misleading and I hope to be able to clear this mess up in the next few pages.

Dick came to my office to work out what he called some "minor marriage difficulties." Dick was twenty-four at the time and had been married for a little under three years. Both Dick and his wife were employed as educators in the local school system. Dick taught high school math and his wife Renee taught in the elementary school. He presented well and was very verbal and likable. Discussion was easy for him and he had a terrific sense of humor. Athletic looking with a masculine six foot physique, he told me that he spends a good deal of time at the gym . After the initial information gathering, I turned it over to him to explain the reason for his visit.

"I think that my marriage needs a bit of help. My wife seems to think that things are just fine but I'm not buying that anymore. Renee is the girl of my dreams. Really I think she'd be the girl of just about everyone's dreams. First of all, she is totally, awesomely beautiful. Secondly she has a body that most women would die for. She's bright, athletic, empathetic and a great listener. Sex is awesome and has never been a problem. We have similar goals and we're totally compatible. Everyone who meets her is struck by her bubbly outgoing personality. Everyone- really everyone- likes her. People we know call us Ken and Barbie. I hate that, but the fact remains that everyone thinks we're the perfect couple. She's everything I've ever looked for in a woman except for that one little annoying habit. Maybe habit is not the right word to use. I think it's more of an annoying behavioral trait or whatever you guys want to call it."

At about this time, I noticed Dick getting upset as if there was a great deal more he wanted to say but he was conflicted. I got us both a glass of water from my mini-fridge and told him to slow down and take his time. After two or three minutes, he continued.

"I have to tell you that for the most part our marriage is wonderful, really wonderful. It's perfect ninety-nine percent of the time. Sometimes, I think that I'm making too much of the one percent. I know you're supposed to have me come up with all the answers and that your job is to guide me through this process but I'd really like an honest opinion if at all possible.

I first became aware of the problem on our honeymoon when we were unable to get the room we wanted at the hotel we had booked. The room they gave us was fine and almost identical to the room we wanted but Renee just couldn't let it go. She began to get angry at the front desk clerk and started to raise her voice. I calmed her down and took her to the room for a glass of champagne. Didn't work. She was getting angrier by the minute even though she knew that the room we wanted was not guaranteed. After a few minutes, she called the front desk and asked to speak to the manager. He came on the line and she unleashed an unbelievable amount of anger on that poor guy. Didn't work. She turned to me and began to berate me for not taking up for her and for not manning up. Again, she was getting angrier and angrier and there was just no conceivable way to calm her down. The episode ended a few minutes later when she picked up a lamp and threw it at me, missing me by inches. To this day, she'll say that she wasn't throwing it at me but I don't believe it. Afterwards, I had to go to the front desk to explain that we accidentally broke the lamp as we were unpacking our bags. A hundred and twenty dollars later I was back in the room. For a while, we just stared at each other. She started to cry and apologized from the bottom of her heart for her behavior which she told me was something that had never happened before. Somehow, deep down, I didn't believe her but I decided to adopt a wait and see attitude. She was remarkably convincing with her apology and I believed that I would not see a replay of that behavior again.

I was so wrong. About three months later, there was an episode at a movie theater when we were unable to get seats directly in the middle of a row. A full-fledged tantrum followed by a sincere apology to me and all the people in the theater followed her outburst. She made an incredibly embarrassing scene and all I wanted to do was disappear. This case was a little different from the honeymoon meltdown. This time, she deliberately threw her soda on me. There was no denying her intent this time as people in the rows in front of us were also covered with soda. Had to get all their telephone numbers so I could pay for the cleaning bills, which I did at the cost of fifty five dollars. We left and she did what she always does. She apologized profusely and reverted to the kind hearted, sweet and adorable woman that I knew.

The way I figure it, she has one of these episodes about one percent of the time. The other ninety-nine percent, she is close to perfect. The problem is that now I'm a little gun shy as I never know when I'll be dealing with the crazy side of her. Did I say crazy? I guess that about says how I feel and my question is am I a little off? Or is there something really, really wrong with her?

Before you answer, I need to tell you about the last episode that happened two days ago. It's a long story so I'll just give you the highlights. We were driving in our van and I was in the passenger seat because she prefers to drive. She started to argue with me about the current state of our country. In particular, our President. These discussions in the past have never ended well so I remained relatively quiet while her insanity escalated to the ozone layer. She was screaming and cursing and morphed into the least attractive person I had ever seen.

She then reached over and started hitting me. Can you believe it? All this over a one sided discussion of our President. I asked her to let me out of the van because I wanted to walk home. She stopped the van and as I was getting out she hit the gas and pushed me out the door. As a result, I have a few scrapes and bruises but I feel that, all in all, I was very lucky.

About fifteen minutes later, here she comes crying and apologizing, asking me to get into the van so she can drive me home. I refused and walked home to be greeted by a cacophony of apologies that I've heard before. I'm ready to leave her but I just needed to bounce this off someone and hearing myself I now know that if she doesn't get some help then I'm adios."

We sat and discussed their relationship and the fact that, in three years, she has shown this behavior ten or twelve times. I told him that he was right to be upset and then we discussed some simple math. In a normal year of three hundred and sixty five days he can expect this behavior approximately every three and a half months. This is obviously totally unacceptable. He had talked to her about her rage in the past and she had chosen to do nothing about it. She felt they were okay because the outbursts were so infrequent. He said to me that he didn't see any of this coming when they first met.

My words of advice were very limited as he had already seen the light and knew that she needed help or the marriage would end. She refused to seek counseling under any circumstances. Shortly thereafter, they divorced. This case brings to mind one of my favorite concepts in psychology which is to be careful who you ask for. You know that wonderful list of characteristics that you wrote for me? Meaningless. It's not the good stuff that leads to poor relationships. It's the bad stuff that you never saw coming. Or it could be the bad stuff that you chose to ignore. It could even have been something that you thought you could change. The list that everyone should make is a list of the deal-breakers. These are the issues that will prove to be intolerable in the long run. Unfortunately, many of these issues are well hidden at the beginning of relationships and emerge slowly over time. Think about the first time you loudly belched in front of your paramour. I'll bet it wasn't on the first or second date. What if now, a year later, you find that he or she absolutely delights in high decibel belching and you can't stand that disgusting noise. Is it a deal breaker? In many cases, it would be. In some cases, it would have to elevate to profound flatulence before the deal is off. More than half of all marriages end in divorce and the only way I know to reasonably insure success is to wait until you're absolutely sure that you know that person. The second factor is as important as the first and I'm sure that I will be the first psychotherapist to come up with this concept. You need to be able to communicate. Whether you're dating or married forty years, you need to be able to effectively communicate with each other. Pretty profound huh?

Think about the issues that break up relationships and, again, be aware that most of these issues aren't evident at the beginning of our love affairs because we are so blinded by the good. What are some of the changes that could pop up and become future issues. Let's look at some.

- Either partner decides that having children is not a good idea.
- Either partner becomes bored with sex and would prefer to read a book at night or get on the computer.
- One of the partners has a very cute habit of popping their gum but, by the second year, you want to put the gum in a place where it should not go.
- He decides to stop work and be a professional photographer.
- She decides to become an actress and wants to move.
- She loves pets and wants six cats... He likes dogs.
- One partner is going to school at night while the other partner is watching Game of Thrones
- Weight gain... Weight loss
- Incredibly annoying family members
- One partner wants to save money and the other partner loves to spend.

You get it. Relationships are difficult. Even apparently perfect relationships need a periodic tune up. If you don't have the ability to effectively communicate then you have lost your ability to have a productive tune up. If you don't allow yourself the requisite amount of time to really get to know someone, you are in for a hell of a surprise, or surprises. Be careful who you ask for.

17. SO WHO'S SENDING THE TORNADO?

Three men are riding in separate cars along a rural road in Kansas in a very bad storm. At approximately the same time, they see a monstrous tornado coming towards them. All three men drive to a house about a mile up a narrow road to escape the twister where a woman graciously lets them in. Peering out the windows, they see that the tornado has doubled in size and is heading directly towards them. The three men and the woman huddle in a closet and cover themselves with a mattress. As the skies continue to darken and the winds pick up one man starts to pray to Allah, his God. The second man, a Christian, starts to prey to his God saying, "Save me Jesus." The third man, hearing all the praying, bows and begins to pray to his Shinto God. The woman sits quietly under the mattress and watches them without uttering a word. After a few minutes, one of the men asks her why she's not praying for God to save her. She looks at the man and says, "Who do you think is sending the tornado?"

This story tends to upset some people who make a distinction between God and the devil. These people feel that they are two separate entities and that it is the devil that is putting the group in harm's way. Regardless of your personal thoughts, religion brings out both the best and the worst in many people.

There are around four thousand two hundred religions in the world today. Christianity takes the title as the largest and Islam follows in second place. Other religions exist around the world and we are totally unaware of the great majority of them. The following are some of the religions that you may be unaware of. They include; Shinto, Taoism, Ajivika, Charvaka, Jainism, Druze, Yazdanism, Faism, Fallin Gong, Cao Dai, Soto, Kegon, Smartism, Shakers and a whole slew of others.

Some religions are so obscure that they border on the ridiculous. These include Vampirism, The Church of Euthanasia, Raelism (a UFO religion), Jedism (maintaining Jedi rights), Pastafarianism (worshippers of the flying spaghetti monster) and Frisbeetarianism (a belief that your soul goes on your roof when you die until someone gets a long stick and knocks your poor soul down).

Joe's story will give you an idea of the complexities of religion. He came to my office to discuss difficulties he was having with his girlfriend of a year. I'll let you hear for yourself.

"I'm twenty nine and my girlfriend Marie is twenty-eight. I'm a computer programmer and I've been working for the same firm for seven years. I love my job, I love the people and I love the money. I have no complaints with my life and I feel that I'm in the right place, headed in the right direction. I was married once before to a woman who felt that her role in life was to emasculate and berate me. I call her my transitory intestinal gas release because I sort of knew what she was like but I thought she'd mellow with time like a fine wine. Some people just call it an extended brain warp. Big mistake as over time she turned into a bottle of grape juice. As a result, I've tried to date what I call 'nice' women. I look for women who are devoid of anger and are spiritual although not necessarily religious. I shy away from the crazies with long stories of the men who hurt them and longer stories about what bastards men are in general. I give these women a wide berth because I hate drama with a passion. I'm a realist and drama does not fit well with someone who sees things as they are. One other thing that will be very important as we talk is the fact that I'm Jewish. I'm proud of who I am and I'll defend Judaism to the end but I'm not a real practicing Jew. I observe the holidays but I love shrimp, lobster, pork, bacon and other foods that are supposed to be religiously taboo. I believe that my God will forgive me and my passion for bacon. Deep fried bacon wrapped around a hot dog is perfect. After all, doesn't God want me to be happy? I was standing in line in a deli about a year ago waiting to order a pastrami Reuben and a potato knish when I noticed a very attractive woman standing behind me. After I ordered, I listened to what she was ordering and to my surprise found that she was also going to have a pastrami Reuben with a potato knish. Call it kismet or whatever you want but that started us on our journey which brings me here today. She admitted later on in the day that she had never eaten either a Reuben or a knish but she thought I was cute and ordered so that she could chat me up. Ain't it funny how things work out?

We started to go out the next night and she was wonderful in every way. She was, and still is what I call nice. There's was no drama, no anger and despite a previous divorce, no hatred towards men. She did have an eight year old boy who is a terrific little kid and we got along famously. Marie and I loved to talk and we spent hours sitting on the couch chatting with each other. Sex was great from the start until we hit a roadblock when it came to intercourse. It seems that she wanted a grand commitment before she would do what she called the nasty deed. I, on the other hand wanted to make sure that we were sexually compatible before I signed my soul away. So, we started to struggle until the real reason for her reluctance came out and this is where the problem lies.

Marie was a devout Roman Catholic. When I say devout, I mean church at night during the week and always on Sunday. I mean a woman who will not eat a meal- any meal- without saying Grace. This included holding hands and bowing our heads in Burger King, McDonald's, Arby's and upscale restaurants such as the Beach Bistro. I was feeling a tad uncomfortable as the whole Jesus thing was being forced down my throat. We realized that we would need to find a common ground when it came to religion. This realization sent us on a quest to find a religion and a church that we could both accept. Every Sunday, we would find a new church and go to their services. We have gone to churches where they speak in tongues and we have gone to churches where not a word is spoken in English. You name it and we've done it. We both realized that we probably would need to go to a non-denominational church that centers more on spirituality and not dogma. Seven non-denominational churches in a row and we were back at square one.

We visited a total of twenty two houses of worship in twenty two weeks. It was a God awful frustrating experience for me but I wanted to try to give it my best. Marie found something wrong with every church and I began to realize that we could look for years and never find a church to her liking. Sex was really becoming an issue for me as she refused to have intercourse but strangely all other kinds of sex were okay. That's one weird religion that permits nudity and oral sex but prohibits intercourse. The end result is that I felt that it was either her way or no way. Everything came to a head recently when we were discussing our favorite topic- religion.

Sitting at our customary couch, she told me that she has no problem with my being Jewish if we could only be yoked. Yoked. What the hell was yoked? She explained to me that she believed that, in order, for a couple to flourish and achieve their highest potential, they must be yoked. Without 'yoking', a word I just made up, she said we could never be equal. And then the turd hit the proverbial fan. She told me that you need two oxen to pull a wagon and they need to pull equally. If one ox leads and one follows then they are not equal and the relationship cannot work. So, I asked her if I'm the one who is behind and is she the superior oxen in the lead and she said yes. What it came down to is that if I did not become a follower of the same religious ideals that she held, I would be holding up the fucking ox train. Wow.

This last conversation took place about three weeks ago. At the end of the conversation, I told her that I was done and that she needed to find another ox. I was angry and I really wanted some payback to repay her for thinking that she could place herself above me. Who does that? My immature self from my teenage days took over about then and, despite the fact that she told me that we could work around our problems, I knew we were finished. Totally and completely done. We dated for two more weeks and, in a very non-subtle way, I started to let her have it. I tormented her continually that entire time. I would hum Jewish folk songs and I started to wear my yarmulke everyplace we went. When we would talk, I would use expressions such as "Oy vey" or I would suddenly start dancing and singing "Hava Nagila." I told her that I only wanted to eat in Jewish establishments from then on and I would only order matzoh ball soup and gefilte fish even in a pizzeria. I asked her to the movies and told her that I wanted to see the Ten Commandments five times. It's funny that during those two weeks, the lack of sex didn't bother me at all.

Finally, I realized that I had gone far enough and that I had made my point. I decided to cut her loose, after all she really was kind of nice, except for that one little problem. What surprised me is how strongly she felt about breaking up. I believe that she felt that given enough time that I would elect to leave my Neanderthal ways, stand upright and join the other Roman Catholics. I ended our last night with a prediction and I told her a story. I told her that I had a vision of the two of us approaching the Pearly Gates of heaven. I told her that I went first and was immediately admitted on a platinum level, not even the gold level I had hoped for. I told her that when she went to the gate, she was assessed by a hundred year old rabbi who just looked down at her and said, "Oy vey, did you make a mistake!" The story had the desired effect as we parted on my terms as I am now the lead ox and she has a half a yoke."

Religion is a deal breaker and despite four thousand, two hundred religions, some people believe that they have it right and everyone else is wrong. Statisticians would laugh at the odds but that's where faith comes in and overrules everything. Faith is a complete trust or confidence in someone or something. Furthermore, it is a belief in God or doctrines of religion that is not based on truth. Truth, in this case, can be construed as hard evidence. In other words, you should not need hard and fast proof to believe, you just believe. It has been noted by cynics through the years that one's faith exists to make certain that you have a place in the afterlife. Not just a place, but a really good place with running water, good French food and fine wine. This is where many people go off the rails and fall into the realm of hypocrisy. The Jew who fasts for Yom Kippur and does nothing else during the year feels he or she has fulfilled their religious obligation. The weekly church goer has a reserved front seat in the clouds up high. I don't think so. I believe that the answer lies in spirituality and not in the number of cakes you sell at the church bazaar.

What is spirituality and why do we have such a hard

time being spiritual? A spiritual person is someone whose highest priority is to be loving to oneself and others. They care about people, animals, the planet and they are kind. Not so difficult you think? In actuality, this is very hard to achieve. This brings me to Grace, a woman misnamed from birth.

I worked with Grace for three years while I was a consultant for a large manufacturing company. Grace was the administrative assistant and personal accountant to the owner and, as such, wielded a great deal of power. On the surface, Grace was, at age sixty, a wonderfully devout religious woman who was revered by her local church.

Constantly collecting money for one good cause after another, she was the epitome of a righteous and spiritual woman. She attended church on Sundays and usually two other nights during the week. She was on every committee possible and was visible throughout the community. Once a month, she would have the two priests from her church for dinner and their birthday celebrations were legend. What a gal. The dark side is that Grace was a fanatic for power and to cross her in any way meant that you would pay a price- in spades. I personally saw her in action numerous times. To slight her was akin to waking a rabid dog.

I saw her undermine workers that she did not favor on a regular basis. She would misinform the owner about a number of issues to the detriment of others. I heard her lie about a number of incidents that I had observed first hand. I saw her change the time card of a worker because she didn't like him. She was toxic and pure poison to everyone around her but the owner was oblivious to what was going on. Grace also felt that the Cubans and the Puerto Ricans were a small step above heathens and would treat them like dirt. Grace got under my skin and began to bother me more and more but to confront her one on one would have definitely ended my consultant position. I decided to confront her with the owner in the room as I would rather have lost my position than to stay and watch her perform her nasty work.

At our meeting, I reviewed eight incidents for the owner that put Grace in a very poor light. I reviewed each incident calmly and Grace denied each one as they were discussed. My ace in the hole was the fact that I had already talked to the five people involved in the incidents and asked if they would be willing to talk to the owner if I initiated this meeting. To my surprise, they all said yes. They were called into the room individually and each reported what Grace had done to them.

Grace became quieter and quieter as the meeting progressed until she couldn't take it anymore and just left. I felt sorry for her but her days as Queen of the Nile were definitely over. She returned to work the next day and the owner had a two hour meeting with her where I was told she shed a thousand tears. I'm not really proud of what I did but her behavior changed from that day onward. I believe it was due to what the owner called her. He told her that she was a hypocrite of the worst order and that she should be ashamed of herself, and she was. She remained in her position which I believe was the right decision.

Saying the right words and doing the right things does not make you a good person. Living a spiritual life filled with love and compassion is probably the way to go. I left the firm two years after that momentous day and Grace and I got along famously. Something had changed in her but I would never really be able to trust her. I even hugged her goodbye when I left making sure of course that she didn't stick a kick me sign on my back.

Many therapists spend the bulk of their time with their patients trying to review the past to determine how and when their difficulties began. I know therapists who will spend a year or two trying to find answers to questions that have no bearing on their patients getting better. The reality, the base truth is that you always get to a point in therapy where you have to do something. Doesn't depend upon your past or what got you to where you are. The fact is that here you are and you need to do the work to make an effective change in your life. Yes, your brother beat you when you were eight and now you're thirty-seven. Yes, you're adopted and you've gone through difficult times feeling abandoned. Let's keep going over your trauma for the next five years in therapy so that we fully understand how you got to where you are. Poppycock, bull turds and horse shit. What if you never find the reasons for your past behavior? Are you doomed? Absolutely not.

In the end, you have to be responsible for who you are and who you want to be. You need to advocate for yourself and stop hiding behind your ADHD or your loss of a finger or your religion. Of all people, Doctor Seuss said it the best when he said that you have brains in your head. You have feet in your shoes. You can steer yourself any direction you choose. It's time to start walking.

18. MY CHILD IS THE BRIGHTEST, PRETTIEST AND MOST ATHLETIC NINE-YEAR OLD IN THE SCHOOL

During my years of private practice, I found that I preferred to work with older adolescents or adults. I worked wit children for more than twenty years and found that adults were much more likely to have meaningful insight and subsequent behavioral changes. I also found that the most effective way to work with children is to work with the parents. A child is with his or her parents or in school for most of the week except for the fifty minutes that I had the child in therapy. I believe that they needed to know how to deal effectively with their child to gain the skills needed to be an effective parent.

Julia came to see me when she was a sixteen year old high school junior having a number of problems. Both in school and out. She was crushed when she didn't make the cheerleading squad and alienated many of her friends by accusing them of being granted favoritism. She was having ongoing battles with two of her teachers who she claimed were being unfair when they marked her tests.

Finally, she was having a range of social problems ranging from being excluded from parties to not being able to hold onto a boyfriend.

She told me that the only people in the world who understood her were her parents. She loved the fact that her mother would go to battle for her anytime there was a need. It was her mother who gave the captain of the cheerleading squad an earful of anger because she wasn't chosen. It was Mom who went to the Principal to complain about the two teachers who were treating Julia so unfairly. It was Dad who called the parents of the teenagers who did not invite her to the parties to try to straighten all that out. What the heck was going on?

Julia presented as an average looking sixteen year old who was very vivacious and outgoing. She was verbal to a fault and tended to want to hear herself talk as opposed to listening to anyone else. Her self-esteem was out of the ballpark as she felt somewhat superior to everyone, including me. I realized that this was a young lady who had been coddled, pampered and entitled since she was born. She believed that she was a step above everyone else and was totally unable to see how this attitude was alienating her from others. At the age of sixteen, she was mimicking what she had been taught from day one. She was fed a constant diet of praise with very little reality. Whenever confronted with a situation where she did not get what she felt she deserved, she became angry and verbally abusive to others. Her defense was to put other people down. That was her only coping skill. She would talk about their poor choice of clothes, their ugly hair, their shabby homes and even their uneven teeth. If there was something negative to be said, she would say it. It was perfectly clear that these behaviors were causing all the difficulties but how could she possibly believe that her behavior was acceptable?

The answer was simple once you met the parents. We have a phrase in psychology called D.O.A. which means difficult On Arrival. I understand that this phrase is also commonly used in restaurants for very difficult customers. They were difficult from the second they entered my office when they told me that my office was a little bit old, but potentially charming. They established the chain of command immediately by asking a number of questions related to my fees and grilled me on the type of therapy that I practiced.

Clearly, they wanted to lead and I knew, after years of practice, to let them lead until they were ready to give up the reins. I've been able, from that time until today, to tolerate a great deal of annoying behavior because I had a secret weapon. If at some point in time their behavior became intolerable and the therapeutic process or I felt violated, I could always fire myself. Working for yourself is a wonderful thing and I have fired myself no less than eight or ten times in forty two years of private practice. Can't file for unemployment insurance. But, it feels just right.

Both mom and dad were overdressed as if they had front row seats at the symphony for a matinee perfor-mance. Mom was homely and a bit on the paunchy side with dark darting eyes that never appeared to stop moving. Dad was slim bordering on delicate and appeared somewhat haggard. He never smiled and spoke in a monotone constantly using words that I was unfamiliar with. He was able to work the words belatron and belaud into his first three paragraphs. I have yet to look up these words but I doubt that I will ever use them regardless of what they mean. In retrospect, I believe that he was working his way through the dictionary to find impressive words and was only up to the letter b. Admirable? I don't think so.

"My daughter told me that she enjoyed your sessions but she would prefer if you allowed her a bathroom break in the middle, if at all possible. I'm sure you can work that out with her during her next session. I'd love to hear what you think but first, I have to tell you some of the history so you can get a better idea of what our Julia is all about. We both love her to pieces but she seems to be getting into a lot of difficulties at school and socially. The school system as a whole is terrible despite their high ratings. They really believe their press and think that their A rating actually means something. Julia has never been challenged and most of the teachers have no true understanding of children or how to teach. We're trying to form a committee of parents to challenge the school system and their curriculum. We also want to change a number of other rules that these poor kids live by but, so far, no other parents want to join us in this battle.

Socially, our Julia seems to be out of the loop mainly because the other kids are downright mean and resentful of her talents and abilities. She is a special, gifted child who always has to deal with less mature girls who conduct themselves like five year olds. The boys are no better and all they seem to want is a quiet non-threatening girl who will have sex with them. Total idiots. I remember when Julia was nine years old and I told her that she was the brightest, prettiest, most athletic nine year old in the school. I've repeated that thought to her probably a hundred times over the years."

There it was! Right out there for everyone to hear. A declaration of stupidity that was destined to cause future pain for our Julia. Mom went on to explain what she felt was her role was as a mother. She felt that the primary job of any parent is to build up their children at all time and in all aspects of their life. Fostering self-esteem was the number one job of a parent with the second role as a protector. As a protector, the parents are to monitor the child's life and intervene and fight the fight, if necessary. This now explained everything. As the consummate helicopter parents, it appeared that behaviors manifested by both Julia and her parents was not about to change in the near future.

Yes, the job of a parent is to protect their children and to build their self-esteem. But, not in the absence of reality. What happens when our Julia tries out for the softball team and doesn't make it? How does she feel when she gets a grade of C on an essay? How crushed will she be when no one asks her to the junior prom? How does she reconcile her elevated self-esteem with the reality of her life? The answer is that it will require a good dose of reality and re-thinking for her to find her place. Julia's parents did her a tremendous disservice by not allowing her to experience a few heartbreaks and disappointments. She was, at the age of sixteen, woefully unprepared to face the world of adolescence. Sometimes too much praise is just not a good thing unless coupled with reality. Unfortunately, the lines between success and failure are becoming blurred as it appears that we never want to hurt a child's feelings.

Recently, I attended an awards assembly in an elementary school. Awards were given out for improvement every quarter. The children in each class were marched onto the stage to receive a certificate of improvement. The initial idea was to have the children all feel good about their accomplishments and their hard work. In every class of twenty-five, there were one or two students who were left in the cafeteria as they were not going to be awarded a certificate. As a result, there was a total of about twenty children who were separated from their classes and made to sit with the other losers from the other classes. That's exactly what the other kids called them. Losers. A tiny step above lepers. Why do people try to reward children for everything that they do while all the kids and the adults already know who are the real front runners. The awards assembly was wrong on a number of levels. Due to the large numbers of children awarded, the certificates lost their meaning. In addition, separating the children from the herd only served to severely damage their self-esteem and had the effect of distancing them from their peers.

I saw Julia for a few weeks but the parents were hell bent on undermining the therapeutic process from the onset. Their belief that their role as the esteem builders and protectors was too strong to budge but I feel that we did make some inroads.

Possibly at some future time, she'll return and both

she and her parents will be open to a dose of the real world. I truly hope so.

There is a fine balance between too much praise and too much reality. You need to encourage and strive to obtain the best in your children but you must take into account both their assets and their liabilities. As a parent, you also run the risk of sounding too negative if you are constantly talking about limitations. Constant negativity could lead to an adolescent or an adult with a fear of failure. These individuals are afraid to take chances as they feel that the end result will be unfulfilling. Taking risks is very difficult for them and they tend to take the comfortable established path through life. They set their goals a little too low and once they achieve them, they are reticent to move on. Life for them takes a path through the rigors of daily living that lacks true excitement.

You also have people who develop a fear of success. These individuals are afraid to move forward because if they do succeed then they will always have to perform at that very high level. It is much easier for them to strive for a simpler attainable goal than to have to perform at their peak level from that point on. You can clearly see this thinking in some mismatched couples.

Marjorie was a remarkably talented physician. She was at the top of her class in both college and med school. In addition, she was both popular and a born leader professionally and personally. She chose to marry a man with a college degree finishing dead last in his class. He had a succession of marginal positions ranging from computer sales to medical sales and finally becoming a physical education teacher. There is nothing wrong with any of the positions per se but there was a good deal wrong with him. He was withdrawn and never wanted to attend functions with her friends because he said that they were too uptight. He shirked his duties around the house and was terrible his handling their finances. After a few years, it seemed that she was the mother to an adult child and she was the only responsible mature party of the two.

Marjorie was never really looking for an equal. She was looking for a relationship with a man who was never going to measure up and never be a rival. She took the easy road and found the perfect man to be with through sickness, health and immaturity. Her husband satisfied her basic needs and, despite his poor work history and asocial tendencies, he was a perfect fit for her. Their relationship became predictable and boring until she progressed rapidly in the medical field while he would never learn to cook, clean, or balance his check book. The disparity was growing as the days passed and finally, Marjorie came to the conclusion that the marriage needed a good deal of help if it were to survive.

That's where I came in. Sometimes, when a new patient comes into my office I can tell the outcome within the first hour. They came in together for the first visit, something that he demanded as I usually see couples separately at first. By the end of the second session, I could sense that Marjorie wanted out of the marriage and that therapy was just a step that she felt was needed along the way to the eventual divorce. At the end of our memorable second session, she told me that she would be coming in to see me alone and that her husband would have to find his own therapist. The end was near as once you open your eyes to this kind of discord in your relationship, you cannot simply close your eyes and make believe that it can go away. She chose him for all the wrong reasons and tried to deceive herself for years but eventually the reality of her life with him was too apparent to dismiss.

Too much praise or too little? If you're at either extreme, difficulties begin to rear their ugly heads. There is a balance between reality and your dreams and goals. There is a danger when there is no balance coupled with a lack of accepting reality. Julia will pay the price for her parent's mistakes until, one day, when she realizes that she's not the best nor does she need to be. We should all have dreams that we pursue as far as humanly possible while at the same time balancing your life. Giving up on your dreams is very difficult but working towards an unrealistic goal can be devastating. Some people refuse to give up their dreams despite years of sweat and tears. I admire them but I worry about them at the same time.

At a mighty five foot seven inches, I still await a call to play back up center for the New York Knicks. Go figure.

19. WHEN DID THE OBESE SEAL ARRIVE?

A number of years ago, a good friend of mine was having some minor difficulties with his pool. As I had similar breakages in the past I offered to help him fix the problems. The only dilemma was that the fact that the water temperature in his pool was about sixty-five degrees. I tend to wimp out when water temps go below eighty degrees. The solution was simple as I had a wet suit that I had used on a vacation ten years prior and that kept me both dry and warm when I entered the Icelandic waters. It took only a few minutes to find the wetsuit but getting into the suit took longer than expected. Much longer. My guess, at that time, was that the suit had shrunk over the intervening years and that it would soon be time to buy a brand new one.

After a brief struggle fitting all my body parts into the suit, I left his bathroom to take the short walk to the pool where my friend was waiting with our respective wives. Walking down the hallway, I glanced to the side. I was amazed to see a giant black seal. I was startled by the sheer size of the behemoth and wondered who in their right mind has a seal as a pet? Slowly backing up so as to not startle the creature, I took a better look.

As I peeked, I realized that my friend had mounted a full length mirror in the hallway and the seal was, unfortunately, me. Couldn't possibly be me because I thought I knew how I looked so I figured that he had one of those distorting mirrors that you find in a fun house. Creeping to the next room and the next mirror, my worst fears were confirmed. It was definitely me. When did the obese seal arrive was all I could think to ask my wife when I went outside. While asking her, I began to flap my flipper like arms together and make seal-like sounds. I was sorely tempted to ask her if I looked fat but I was able to stop myself in time.

We all had a good laugh at my expense which was well deserved. We fixed the pool and on the ride home, I asked my wife why she didn't tell me that I looked so rotund. She told me that she did a number of times. She was right because I remembered her telling me that my pants were getting too tight. She reminded me that she told me that I had the beginning of a bad muffin-top. She then recalled numerous times when I would order a grand unnecessary dessert after a huge meal at a restaurant. She did her part but I just wasn't listening. Sometimes, it's a really good idea to listen to what people say even if it might be a tad painful to hear. All this brings me to Bobby, a fifteen year old male who was having significant trouble with women. I found it difficult to believe that he could have that much trouble with dating at such a young and tender age but, alas, he was.

Bobby was a very articulate young man who looked a number of years older than his fifteen years. He was tall with dark brown hair and could have been a double for Tom Selleck in his youth. I could see how he could drive the young ladies wild. In addition, he had a terrific sense of humor coupled with a wild child personality that many women and young ladies find irresistible. He was immediately likable. The crux of the matter as he told me is as follows.

"I have a lot of girlfriends and I really like them but something happens after we decide to go together as a couple. We have a few good weeks and then, all of a sudden, they break up with me. I'm not talking once or twice. I'm talking like six or seven times in the last year. At first, it didn't bother me but now it's kind of pissing me off because I have to keep finding new girls. It's not hard finding them but I'm really getting tired of all the rejections and I don't understand what's happening. It's like out of the blue, they just suddenly call me or text me or whatever and break up. One girl, Arianna, actually left a sticky note on my math book after class to tell me she didn't want to see me anymore. Most of them don't even talk to me after we break up, or I should say after they break up with me. I don't have bad breath. I don't fart or belch in front of them and I don't have gross body odor. What the hell's going on?"

We talked at length about his dating difficulties and discussed what he would do on a typical date. Everything he told me did not offer a clue as to the cause for the multiple dumpings. I asked him if he ever spoke to any of the girls after a breakup to find the reason why he was continually dumped and he said no. Most of the girls wouldn't talk to him after their short lived love fest so he just moved on to the next failure. I made a suggestion that I thought was wonderful but I doubted that Bobby would be enthralled with it. I suggested that he call at least three of the girls he had dated and ask them to tell him what went wrong. To my surprise, he thought it was a wonderful idea and whipped out his cell phone and his little black book and began dialing. And yes, he did have a worn little black book that he carried everywhere. He began making the calls and with each one he made sure to say that he wasn't angry and he only wanted honesty. The first girl hung up but girls number two, three and four spoke to him

All three had basically the same thing to say. They all felt that he was a great guy and that the first few dates were fun. They all liked Bobby at first and thought that he was wonderful. The problems arose as soon as they were a couple as in going together or going steady. It seems that as soon as they were officially a couple, Bobby's behavior would change. He became bossy and difficult to communicate with. He treated them poorly as if he owned them and just couldn't be bothered with all the niceties. Two of the girls said he became a total jerk and not too pleasant to be around. One girl said it was like a switch was turned and his entire personality changed. Another girl said it was like being in a very bad marriage at the age of fourteen. Who would want that?

I admire Bobby to this day for having the fortitude to find out what was wrong. I also admire how he handled himself with each conversation. He thanked each girl for being honest and, then, he apologized to each of them for his behavior. I believe that he got the answers he needed and, although a little deflated he decided to change his behavior in the future with this new knowledge in hand.

I saw Bobby for a few more months to determine where that unacceptable behavior came from. It appears that he was mimicking the marriage that he saw at home and was acting exactly as his father acted toward his mother. I am happy to report that his next girlfriend was still with him after three months, a lifetime to a fifteen year-old. You have an obligation to listen to other people and decide if what they say is valid or not. Had I listened, there never would have been an obese seal. Because Bobby listened he stopped being dumped and lost his jerk title.

Not only do you need to listen to others, you need to be aware of the world that you're living in. Awareness of customs and mores will save you from uncomfortable social situations. Here are a few examples to ponder. Do not squeeze the fruit at a market in Italy. It is taboo and the proprietor will yell and curse at you. Do not honk your car horn in the Azores as it is considered extremely rude, and I mean extremely- to the point of bringing on a good deal of anger from other drivers. Be careful driving in California as the motorcycles ride on the broken lines. Should you not yield, once again, you will be dealing with a situation that will be at best, uncomfortable. Try to gauge your surroundings as best as you can, be it in another country or in the next town. The best way to accomplish all of this is to take as much information in before you act. Be an observer and a follower until you

LEN TABICMAN

can determine the appropriate behavior for that particular location at that time.

Bill was a fifty-one year old restaurant manager in Tampa, Florida. He came to see me because he wasn't happy with his life situation and, in particular, his marriage. Bill will now speak for himself.

"This is my second marriage and it looks like it's heading to the shitter. My first marriage ended four years ago after a divorce that took over two years only because of my bitchy ex-wife. My first wife was domineering to the point that she eventually had control over everything, especially me. She handled the finances, the vacations, all the day to day operations, meals, parties, you name it. It was easier to give in than to fight because she was so tenacious and nasty she could simply outlast me in any argument. We used to fight over raising the kids until I realized that she could argue straight through the night and then start fresh again in the morning. It was a horrible twelve years and I couldn't wait for the marriage to end. She torments me now whenever she can even though I minimize our contacts.

My wife now, number two in a series of disasters, is a carbon copy of my first rodeo. She is domineering in every area of our lives and it seems to be getting worse every day. Same story as the first wife. She controls everything in our lives and, once again, I feel like I'm suffocating. The other day, I had to ask, no that's not true. I didn't ask. I had to beg for more lunch money. We were having a special lunch at work to celebrate birthdays and I needed fifteen dollars more for the lunch and the gifts. You would have thought that I was going to buy the god dammed crown

166

jewels the way she carried on. What are the odds of finding two women so similar when there are millions of women out there? I have a terminal case of bad luck but, in my heart, I knew this would happen. To add insult to injury, my mother was the grand dame of control and dominance. If anyone were to ever write a book about control and dominance ,my mother would have written it and her picture would be proudly displayed on the front cover. So, I knew this would happen because these women are attracted to me like bees to honey.

I had a very good friend way back before I married for the first time. We grew up together and he knew my mother very well. He would call her the 'Gestapo Mom' which was funny at the time. Now, not so funny. He told me that I was doomed and that I would always look for dominating women like my mother. I laughed when he told me this but, as it happens, he was right on target. The question I have to answer is whether or not I attract them or do they attract me. Really doesn't make a hell of a difference because the result is the same. Why didn't I listen? Why didn't I at least take his words under advisement? The bottom line is that I'm in for a shitload of bad times, money poorly spent and grief if I try to disentangle from my new Himmler."

Why didn't he listen is a good question. Why don't most people listen is a good question. Part of the answer is that we like to hear ourselves talk and we're not that crazy about listening. One of my professors in graduate school said something that I felt was profound to this day. He said that we already know what we know and what we want to say so why not listen to the other person to gain a different point of view. Think about it, you're only repeating what you already know and closing down to others. Sad. There are those about us, although small in numbers, who really listen. I was talking to an African American patient of mine a few years ago with the unlikely name of Relur, which actually is ruler spelled backwards. Don't ask me to explain this as I have no real answer but I have some educated guesses. We were discussing the idea of listening and he told me that he felt that he was an excellent listener and that he could give me three good examples of his listening skills.

"I dated a woman a few years ago who was just about ideal for me. We shared the same interests, the same values and we both had a very positive view of the world and our place in it. She was attractive and sex was off the rails. We sat one night and just talked for eight hours about everything and nothing. Everything was headed in the right direction until fucking North Carolina. I see the way you're looking at me and if I were the therapist I would stare also. North Carolina? The woman in question was Sybil and she had a true love for the outdoors. She adored hiking and would walk anyplace. She even parked at the end of parking lots to get more walking in. Her favorite place in the world to both walk and hike was near Lexington, North Carolina. Little by little, she would casually drop hints about living there full time. At first, I thought she was half joking and didn't say much but, after awhile, the hints turned into trying to talk me into the idea of possibly moving. I live in a great house on the water on Tampa Bay with the best view in the universe.

I'm happy with where I am. Why in God's name would I want to move?

After a few months, she became relentless and would discuss the wonders of North Carolina as if she were working for the chamber of commerce. Then, suddenly, one morning after incredible sex, she told me that her goal was to move within the next two years to a cabin in North Carolina near a little stream. This was stated as an absolute and there would be no denying her this dream she held close to her heart. I listened very carefully to her reasoning and her wishes and came to a stark realization. I realized that if I continued to see her then total heart-break was definitely programmed into my future. So I broke up with her that day and actually felt quite relieved to remove potential deer ticks and spiders from my future.

Was she pissed? Hell yes. Does she hate me to this day? Probably. All I did was listen to what she said and take her at her word. I listened and I'm glad that I listened or we'd probably be fighting to this day. I can hear her telling me that I knew that she wanted to move from the beginning of our relationship. I have to confess that I really cared for her and missed her like crazy at first but I decided to take care of myself. That's my number one story and here is number two.

I play basketball with about ten other guys once a week. It's a fun game and our skills range from some good schoolyard players to a few guys who played college ball. Whenever we finish playing, we always go to this little hamburger place for their well-known cheeseburgers. We stay for an hour or so and talk about a range of subjects ranging from the weather to football and everything in between. No politics, no religion and no sexist banter.

One day, right in the middle of our meal, one of the guys, a relative newcomer, said the following out of the blue. He said, "I don't like people." His remark immediately made everyone thoroughly uncomfortable. He didn't offer any further discussion or explanation. Just the fact that he didn't like people. Well, you know what? I consider myself people and took it to heart. To this day, he still plays ball with us but most of us people give him a wide berth as we were totally unsure of where he's coming from. We're not being mean. We're actually listening to what he said and slightly modifying our behavior. Do I think he'll show up one day with an AK-47 and mow us down? I don't think so and I certainly hope not but you never know. Hence the wide berth. I find that I always look for the closest exit when he's around.

My third listening example concerns a neighbor of mine and a boat. I'm fortunate to have a boat. Not a yacht. A boat that I keep on a lift in my backyard. When you have a boat, one of the things that you do is you take people out for a few hours. Sometimes for a full day. On one of those fateful days, I had my neighbors out for an afternoon ride. We all got along famously and I spent a good deal of time with them. Both on the water and on dry land. We were talking about boats and I asked them why they didn't have a boat since they enjoyed boating so much. I should mention at this point that the wife had consumed three or four martinis when she told me that they "like to use other people's money." Not a big deal and not earth shattering by any means.

But, wait a minute. Does this mean that they're using my money? Does this mean that every time he comes to borrow my edger or my power washer or my trimmer that he's using my money? Yes, it does. We remain friends but they will never cruise on my gas-guzzling mini-yacht again. In addition, when he comes to borrow something, which he does at least once a week, I seem to be using it or it's broken. Does this sound childish and immature? Maybe, but I like to use my own money.

Finally, there's the couple that said something so ridiculous that when I heard it, I believed that they were kidding. Once again, it was a simple declarative sentence with a plethora of hidden meanings. All they said was that they have no common sense. What the hell does that mean? They're a great couple and fun to spend time with but the lack of common sense is prevalent and shows itself in many ways. I make allowances for their behavior and try not to get thrown off by some of the things that they do and say. But, the bottom line is that they said it and I have listened.

You should know yourself and you should listen. Even if it's truly painful you should get feedback from others. I hope that the next chapters will offer some assistance in finding out who you are and where you're headed.

20. WHAT DO YOU WANT TO BE WHEN YOU GROW UP?

"Hi. We're really new at this therapy thing so you're gonna have to kinda tell us what to do. I imagine that we sit together on this couch and just tell you what's going on, right? So here goes. My wife and I have been married for fourteen years and we seem to be fighting more and more. I think I'm right and she always thinks that she's right and I kinda give in cause I just can't handle the fighting all the time. I have a bit of a temper but she's in the end zone when it comes to anger."

"I love it when he paints me out as the bad one. We both get angry but I think he walks around angry and grumpy all the time. He gets up in the morning in a bad mood and goes to bed every night in the same damn mood. I shouldn't say every night because if there's a football game on, he actually cheers up until his damn Bucs lose and then he's in a worse mood. Thank God I'm asleep when the game ends so that I don't have to hear his ranting."

I did not feel at that time that this was going to be a

real fun experience for me full of joy and love. Not. Two people who fight constantly and are at odds with each other about everything. I explained the basic rules of therapy to them and told them that they should allow the other person to speak his or her mind. We also discussed attempting to leave the anger at the door and to proceed with an open mind. Then, I asked them to start over and to give me their individual background and view of the problems. And so he began.

"As I said before, we've been married for fourteen years. We both graduated from high school and we have three kids, all boys. Our boys are six, nine and twelve and they all go to the local public school about three miles away from our home. I work six days a week as a plumber's apprentice and my wife works six days a week prepping food in a nursing home. I should say that she works five and a half days cause' she works half a day on Saturday. Our week is hell from the beginning to end. It starts on Monday morning prepping lunches and checking homework. Then, we drive the kids to school and wind up getting home at six or seven every day. Then, there's dinner and clean up, homework for the kids and laundry. We're wiped out every night and the only night I'm up after nine is on Monday night to watch football. Then, we have the weekend and we work around the house all day Sunday and half of Saturday. We also drive the kids to their friends, to the movies, to the mall and any other damn place they need to go. We have one car and I get to use a truck from work so we're wearing out our ten year old car. Soon it's just gonna' die on us."

"Excuse me, honey, can I get a few words in here?

Money is a problem and always has been. Every time we try to save a little, something happens. Last month, our youngest had to have two teeth pulled at a cost of four hundred dollars. The month before, I was having some female problems and had to have some tests done. Six hundred dollars! We have insurance but it's terrible and we can't afford dental insurance for five people. He also forgot to tell you that we have two dogs and a cat that weighs sixteen pounds. So, add feeding and walking the dogs twice a day. The bottom line is that, at the end of the week, we're all totally wiped out. Oh and before you ask about sex, let me tell you that we can cover this topic in about three little words. They would be 'little to none.' He gets two weeks of vacation a year. So do I but because of scheduling, we can never get the same two weeks off. I work on the house when I'm off and he does the same thing for his vacation. That's a joke. Calling it a vacation. We might as well just keep on working and get some more money to pay our bills."

It went on like this for quite some time. He complained about her. Then, she complained about him from her perspective. They were in their mid-thirties, a little overweight and totally miserable. They were both right and they were both wrong at the same time. Their life was one continuous stream of misery and they had few resources either financially or psychologically. There was no joy in their lives as they grind was never ending with no light at the end of the tunnel. There wasn't even a candle flickering.

I felt that the first thing that needed to be done was to break the cycle of misery and bring in some joy and happiness. On their third visit, I asked what I thought was a very simple question. I asked them what they did for fun. They sat there and didn't say a word. It was one of those weird out of body moments where you know something is wrong but you don't know what it is. I finally realized that, for some reason, they didn't want to answer me so I asked them again in a louder voice. No response for a second time although they did turn in their seats to face each other.

I had no idea whatsoever what was going on so I asked them to explain the difficulty with the question. After another minute, which felt like an hour, he looked at me and said that they don't do anything for fun. It seemed that fun was not in their schedule and had not been for years and years. Instead they chose a life of drudgery where unhappiness stretched to the horizon. The concept of fun was lost a long time ago if it was ever once there.

What a life for those poor kids growing up in a home lacking joy and fun. We reviewed their schedules and their financial situation to try to find something that they could do that would be financially feasible. We came upon the idea of freeing a Sunday and spending it at the beach which was free and no more than five miles away. The plans were made and everyone was looking forward to a beach day.

As in everyone's life, sometimes, unexpected things happens. As this is the case, I now have some good news and some bad news. Therapy was very beneficial in the long run and some happiness was able to creep into their lives. After a while, they fought less and started to look forward to things. Fate however is a fickle little thing.

When they left my office to go to the beach the next Sunday, they were smiling, almost beaming. The next week, when they returned from their beach escapade, he was on crutches, bandaged from his ankle to his thigh on his right leg. It seems that his childhood exuberance at the beach led him to jump from a dock onto an oyster bed cutting his leg very badly. I felt a little responsible but they seemed to take his injury in stride and only talked about the wonderful beach day. Too many people live in a treadmill similar to this couple and are unaware of their unhappiness as they take it in stride.

Take a sheet of paper and number it from one to five. On this paper, list your short term plans for the future. By short term, I mean this next week or possibly two, maybe even three weeks, into the future. This list can include plans to go out to parties, dinners, movies, parks, amusement parks. It can also include family outings if they are things that you are looking forward to. These are the positive plans that you have. Do not include dental visits and the like. On another sheet of paper, number from one to five and list your intermediate plans for the future. Intermediate plans usually are plans (positive) that can go as far as a year or two into the future. On your third sheet, you knew there'd be a third, list no more than three goals that you have for the distant future. This third category relates to things that you hope to accomplish over an extended time and could be very much like a wish list. This could be plans for a major trip, to get training, a degree or anything that will change you for the better in the future. The third category is the one that will normally cause the most difficulty if you have never done a self-assessment of where you are now. I would suggest that you take some time now and evaluate where you are in life and just how content you are. This will make category three much easier for you.

You should have three lists in front of you that you can review now along with me. The first thing to note is whether or not you have something on each list to review. If you are lacking anything on your short term plan/goal list, the next few weeks will appear to be relatively boring and unfulfilling. If you're missing items on the second list then you are facing a few months of relative calm and boredom. However, it's the third list that is by far the most important. Your long term plans and goals can have an effect on your short and mid plans. If you're working towards a significant long term goal, you may have to modify short term goals that give intermediate pleasure.

Everyone, regardless of age, sex, nationality, religion and heritage needs to have long term plans and goals. Ask yourself why you are living? Ask yourself what your goal in life is? Picture what will be written on your gravestone at the end of your life. I've had patients sit down and write their obituary in an attempt to have them self-evaluate. I've had patients ask other people to write their obituary to get some legitimate feedback with some meaning. Take some time and take a good look at yourself and then decide to change. Make plans for next week, next month and next year if at all possible.

My wife once said something to me that struck all the right chords. Twenty years ago, we were planning a trip and I thought it would have been best to postpone the trip because we were very busy at that time. She told me that time is a non-renewable resource. Once it's gone, it's gone forever. She was, and still is, one hundred percent right. I could tell you story after story about people who waited for years to travel only to find that their health deteriorated to a point that they were unable to travel when they finally had the money and the time. I could write at length about all the people who put off going back to school until it was too late.

We're here now in this world. We need to find ways to maximize our experiences and our lives while we are able to. We do not want to miss the golden ring as it passes.

Mr. Gutierrez is the poster boy for not waiting. He was a wealthy businessman who owned three restaurants and two grocery stores. At the age of forty-six, he was remarkably successful and very much admired and well-liked by just about everyone. Mr. G was in turmoil because he was in love with a woman and paralyzed with fear. He was afraid that she would reject him. He was afraid to open himself up to her. He was deathly afraid to even consider having an intimate relationship with her. There was something about her that intimidated him to his core.

It should be noted that he was not like this with anyone else. Male or female. In therapy, we tried to figure out what it was about this woman that produced such an effect in him. I encouraged him numerous times to, at least, take a first step and ask her on a date. Or for coffee. Or for anything. But, he was unable to do anything. After a while, we even stopped trying to figure out why she had such an effect on him and we just centered on his taking a first step.

This went on for a very frustrating three months until

Mr. G came into my office despondent and sad. The woman of his dreams, his future, and his love was dating someone new and it looked like it was very serious. It was. A few months after she started to date the other man, she announced her engagement. This sent my client into a tailspin of depression. He told me he should have and he could have. But, it was too late and there was nothing he could do at that point.

Mr. G lived in regret for some time until he finally met someone he liked. After being burned the first time around he proposed to his new love in record time and was married within a few months. Possibly a little too fast indeed but I knew that I couldn't say anything at that time. A little bit of an overreaction on the part of Mr. G but he was not going to be burned again.

Look at your life. Examine your life. Modify your life or change your life entirely if you feel it is not working. Time marches on.

21. GLORY DAYS

I must admit that, at one time, I was a bit of a Facebook fanatic. I was caught up in the excitement of having hundreds of friends even though I barely knew the vast majority of them. I was so proud of my popularity that I was beaming. However, I began to realize that something was way out of line when I was reading my posts one day. I found that Ephreim Mokolokiini had posted a wonderful picture of his recent seafood meal in Tonga. I also saw that Shyrykka Obiowima posted a picture of her recent trip to the Maldives where she ate raw goat. Rita Friedman posted twenty pictures of her new red couch. What the hell was going on? Who were these people whose names I couldn't pronounce eating foods that looked like porridge and intestines? Most importantly how did I let them become my friends? From that day on, I did not accept any new friends and I began to systematically unfriend anyone whose name I couldn't pronounce or anyone who posted furniture pictures.

After the great unfriending, as I call it, I began to think a little more about what people were posting. As is my nature, I then began to try to understand the reasons for some of the posts. This all brings me to Buffy, one of my good buds on Facebook. Or, as they say in today's language, one of my BFf's. Buffy was in her late sixties and was married for about forty years to a dour sort of man who was close to mute. Her posts included pictures of her at 8,9,10,12,13,14, 16, 18, 22, 25,26 and so on. Other pictures were posted of her wedding, her honeymoon and her first house. There were pictures of her at her club from forty years ago and of her vacations thirty-five to forty years in the past.

Almost everything that was posted showed her in her life at a much younger age and with a much thinner body (sorry!). She was living in the past but the question that comes up is why. Why the past and not the present? To some degree, the answer is related to some degree of unhappiness in the present and a yearning to return to those good old "glory days."

Buffy is not alone by a long shot. Many people live in the past in various other ways. When you meet a glory day individual, they normally tip their hand very quickly. Oftentimes, they refer to something in their past within the first ten or fifteen minutes. They live yesterday's dreams. Not today's and definitely not future dreams. They are consumed with reunions, music from their past and old friends. They are joyous when reliving many of their old experiences. If you're a fan of Bruce Springsteen, you may want to listen to his Glory Days song again because it describes the reality of those who live in the past.

There are also individuals who live solely in the present. They live for the moment and plan poorly for the future. They might drink and use drug to excess. They tend to spend much more money than they should. They may have a succession of jobs in their lives and, many times, will not finish tasks. In extreme cases, they may act out to their detriment as they live in the moment.

These people are invariably great to be around. They get invited to parties because they tend to be a lot of fun. So, what's wrong with this you might ask? Everything. They lack planning ability because they lack logical sequential thinking. Logical can be thought of as something that makes sense while sequential refers to putting things in correct order. For example, if I tell you to plan a trip to Rarotonga on your own without a travel agent. What is the first thing that you would need to do? What's the second step and so on? It's the ability to plan a course of action step by step to reach a goal. Some people simply cannot do that.

Finally, we have those individuals living in the future. May I present to you the case of thirty-seven year old Albert. Albert, who did not like to be called Al, presented as a wiry, anxious man who reminded me of Don Knotts. Al (I know he doesn't like Al) was a dreamer and lived for the future. He put away every penny he made for the day when he would spend some of the accumulated wealth. He was single and had never been married. He thought that all women wanted was his money. He shopped for his clothes at Goodwill. He bought food and everything else at Costco. He never vacationed and drove a twelve year old Ford. He very rarely ate out. If he did, it was at a fast food chain. He was living for the future and he expected it to be grand beyond his wildest dreams.

Had he thought this whole thing out? Not really. Did he have anything resembling a plan for his future? Not really. He felt that the future would afford him the happiness and joy that was now missing in his life. He thought that a new life with enough money would do him quite well in the future. Unfortunately, an old saying comes to mind, "No matter where you go, there you are." He was living in the future and not enjoying the moment. He would, undoubtedly, carry his frugality well into his next life chapter. Planning for the future is extremely important. Living in the future and negating the present is a shallow existence.

So, there you have it, the past, the present and the future. The only three places that you have to choose to live. Most people choose without thinking about it. Obviously, a balance is needed. But, what balance is best if you want a fuller life?

For nineteen years, I taught a number of psychology courses at a university in New Jersey. Most of my students were in their late teens and early twenties. I would ask my students about the past, present, future balance. More recently, I taught at a university in Florida with a population of students. Most of them were forty to seventy-five years old. I asked the same question. I'll call the younger students my northern group. and the older Florida group the southern group.

The northern group felt that the balance should be

twenty percent past, thirty percent present and fifty percent future. There was a wide variation of individual responses. But, for the most part, these numbers represent the group at that time. My southern group rated the past at twenty-five percent, present fifty per cent and future at twenty-five percent. The discrepancy between the groups is enormous. But what's more important is how far an individual falls from the group nor. The balance of the three places is dependent upon circumstances, age and a myriad of other variables. There is a generalized norm for every age group. A balance based upon your particular circumstances is the key to mental health.

Where do you find yourself? Where is that position relative to others? Look at the balance of the three factors and rate yourself in each area. If you're happy with the results, you need to go no further. If you're not satisfied with your results, you need to assess your current situation and make some changes. This self awareness of your current status is the first step in the process of readjustment. Once again, honesty is paramount.

The next step is totally up to you as there is no way that anyone, except you, could know your life as it is. This is where there is no way out except doing the work. This could involve a thousand possible changes that could be made to get more in balance with yourself and others.

Once again, this is where reluctance can easily turn into fear. Fear of change, the unknown and a general disruption of your daily habits and lifestyle. At this juncture, it is crucial to make wise choices where you have a range of options.

In 2002, I worked with a man who seemed hellbent on destroying himself. He was a workaholic and was dabbling in a number of different ventures with a sizable number of investments. What he was doing financially seemed reckless but he was as calm as a person could be. He was the same in his personal life. He went from one relationship to another without any drama. One day, I told him that if I lived his life, I wouldn't be able to sleep at night because I'd worry about my investments.

He told me that he had a secret and that his secret was available to everyone but most people chose not to follow his path. He said that the secret was to have as many options as possible in every area of life. He felt that the more options you provide yourself, the less stress you will have. We discussed his finances and he told me that he's allowed himself a multitude of options so that if some of his investments hit rock bottom, he would still be okay. He told me that regardless of what happened, he would be much, much better than just okay. He marveled at people who invest in one entity without taking into account the consequences of a failure of that one investment.

Giving oneself multiple options was the only way for him to live a stress free happy life devoid of worry. In the past, he worked for a large investment firm for more than ten years and was a rising star. Working more than sixty hours a week for those years, he was heavily invested in their retirement program and the future of the company. It never occurred to him to look for another position because he felt that he was on track heading to a bright future. He didn't either refine his skills nor did he look to gain additional skills as the proverbial rainbow was just down the road.

One day, in the midst of a snowstorm, appropriate weather for that ominous day, he found that he was locked out of his office. He found that he was also locked out his building along with hundreds of coworkers. It seems that the company had gone bankrupt after a two year investigation by the I.R.S. and the S.E.C. Neither he nor anyone else on his level was aware of any ongoing investigation. Everyone believed that the new faces in the accounting department were related to the annual audit. They were all wrong.

At the end of the day, he was allowed to enter the building and take his personal effects from his office. He was not allowed to take one sheet of paper related to the company. As a result of the bankruptcy, at least seven very influential people went to jail. This was no consolation for my friend. My friend had lost everything including his pension and his financial investment in the company. The future was pulled out from under him in the space of one day. It took him the better part of three years to get out from under financially and he made a decision that he would never place himself in a position where he was that vulnerable for the rest of his life.

A wiser man after his fall, he summed up his philosophy in three simple words. Never be afraid. Giving oneself as many options as possible takes the fear out of living. Should something go wrong, as things invariably do, then your world will not be turned upside down. Wiser words were never spoken except perhaps when my mother told me not to stick a fork into the electric outlet.

The bottom line is to first determine where you live (past- present-future). The second step is to provide oneself with as many options as possible so that when things go wrong, the effect is minimal. You can't help but be surprised by things that happen in your life but you should never be afraid. Never.

22. OH MY GOD, IS THAT ME?

Over the forty-two years that I practiced psychotherapy, I have been lucky to meet some of the nicest people in the universe. Unfortunately, I have also run across some truly despicable individuals that I felt I would be unable to help in any way. These people could be regarded as well beyond normalcy. They had neither the desire nor the skills to change their behavior. Sounds negative but, in all honesty, when I feel that I need a strong drink after I finish with a patient, there's something very wrong.

Of all the people that I saw in practice, one stands out head and shoulders above the rest on the contemptible scale. The only way to convey his vileness would be to give you a few snippets from our first and only session. I won't even dignify him with a name and will refer to him simply as F. F was thirty three years old and worked in the construction field. It appears that his father had done the same work and brought him into the field. I never found out exactly what he did in construction but it really doesn't matter. He was about six feet tall with a muscular build which was very evident as he was wearing a very tight black muscle shirt. His arms were covered with tattoos and they all appeared related to concepts such as freedom, love and America. He wore his hair in a crew cut and he looked like a bouncer from a very tough nightclub in the roughest section of town. He spoke loudly and with great authority and I felt that to confront him might not be a real terrific idea. All I can say about his facial features is that he reminded me of Charles Manson. He was threatening in his looks and his manner. I decided that I would have to tread very softly as my wrestling skills were poor at best. Many of the things that he said I do not like repeating even though they are not my words so I will leave blanks for you to fill in when necessary, here goes.

"I just gotta tell you, from the start, that the only reason I would ever come to a shrink would be if my girl made me come and she did. I don't think I've got any psycho problems but my girl says we're done if I don't talk to someone. I work in construction and I'm thirty three. Graduated high school and workin' now at the same place for seven years. My girl and my dad said that this couldn't hurt so here I am to be shrunk.

She thinks that I'm too angry but I think I'm okay. I just don't like a lot of things that are goin' on in this country. I also think most people are full of shit and that they need to wake up. I'm sick of so many things that I wanted to make a list for you to read, but I forgot. What's the deal with these emigrants' or immigrints' that are comin' to our country? I think we have enough rag heads or nasty towel heads. Why do we need them Arabs here? Why don't they stay where they are and cover their ugly faces? Those women are so bad looking they need to cover themselves. And how about them little taco eaters from Mexico with their shitty food and dumb music? Do we need them here? I don't think so. I would build a wall and give every border guard a machine gun to kill any of those little s-- that tries to cross the border.

I'm also tired of the blacks ruining this country with their crime and complaining about everything. Was a time years ago when they knew their place but now they want it all. They're just a bunch of n---who should be taken back to Africa on a sinking ship. Serves them right. Then, you got your Jews who own everything and think they're hot shit. All the Jews in Israel should be bombed to hell. Those good Catholics aren't any better all they do is abuse kids and, then, hide behind their religion. I'd like one of those priests to try something with me, he'd be sorry. I'd turn him into a girl and stick -- ------ his -------. I have a bumper sticker on my truck that says, "Abstinence makes the church grow fondlers."

But, what really pisses me off more than anything else is fat people. They act like they're not fat and disgusting and want you to like them for themselves and not for what they look like. Bullshit. I got eyes and I can see. I say that fat is fat and if you can't lose some weight then you need to live in a pigpen with the other shit. Go to the beach and look at them. They look like beached whales flounting- Is that the word? Flounting?- all their blubber. Tubs of shit that we're supposed to pretend are just fu----g beautiful."

Poor F went on at length about black people, northerners, English people, Germans and even Latvians. It was painful to listen to and I prayed that the second hand would move faster to end my time in hell. I would try to stop him numerous times from his ranting to get him on track and to see if there was the slightest chance that he could be successful in therapy. There was not a glimmer of self-reflection nor was there any possibility of insight. He would never change because he had an absolute inability to look at himself. In addition to this, I despised the man and his values. At the end of the session, I told him that there was no charge for the first visit and he was a bit surprised at this. I told him that my schedule was very full and it might be months before I could schedule him in on a regular basis. I referred him to a community mental health clinic where there were four security guards in the building. He was a challenge that I refused to take on. I fired myself and scheduled to call him for a follow-up visit in May of 2035.

You must have the ability to self-evaluate your behavior if there is to be any change. If you are unable to look at yourself objectively then you will be unable to change. How do you do this? Previously, in a former chapter, you were asked to list ten characteristics of yourself and that would be a good place to start. Normally, people can write six to eight characteristics before getting stuck. The last two or three are very difficult for some and impossible for others. At some point, while you are making your list, you will feel a need to include a few negatives and this will take you out of your comfort zone. This discomfort is exactly where you want to be as you have no need to change the positives.

In order for this exercise to be successful, you need to be totally realistic and brutally honest. What is immensely helpful but frightening is to have another individual list what he or she thinks your characteristics are. Sometimes, this can be a real eye opener and you may be challenged to resolve the differences between your list and others.

The question that should be asked is 'Who am I?' The next part of the exercise is to determine a course of action and to make some changes. This plan that you put in place must be realistic, logical and sequential (remember this?). If you are to be successful, you have to be proactive and future oriented. You cannot dwell on the past and live in regret as that will get you nowhere. What's done is done and cannot be changed. There is no place here for regrets for things that you have done in the past. In reality, we all know this but we drag our luggage around with us forever. Not a terrific idea.

There are two other concepts to keep in mind when evaluating oneself. The first is that what other people say about you is none of your business. Yes, that's right, none of your business. You need to listen to your own story and not be unduly influenced by the negativity of others. You need to live your own life and not the life dictated by rumor mongers or people who are not on your side. In general, there are two types of people. There are those who add to your life and there are those that take away. Make another list (I like lists) and put the people you know on either the add list or the take away. This could prove interesting for you when you realize how much time you spend with people who drain your spirit.

The final concept in this chapter is nothing new and has probably been discussed for centuries. Every self help book written talks about this concept. You've heard it before and here it comes again. Take nothing personally. I would bet that, at some time in man's history, a Neanderthal mother said to her son those wonderful words when the other kids at stone toss ignored him. It was the mother of Napoleon who probably told him to ignore those kids who called him shorty. Why do we have so much difficulty with this? We all understand the concept but something about our ego gets in the way every time.

A friend of mine told me a true story once that puts this all into perspective for me. He worked in Manhattan on the seventy fourth floor of an enormous office building. Every morning, thousands of people would wait for the elevators to arrive and then crowd together like sardines for the ride up to their respective floors. My friend took an express elevator that went from the lobby directly to floors seventy and above. One day, he pushed and squirmed to get on the next car and just was able to get in and turn around, when the doors closed. After a few seconds, he felt something digging into his back but was unable to turn around to see what it was. It was bearable but very annoying and since it was raining that morning he convinced himself that it was someone's umbrella. My friend told me that as the elevator went up he became angrier and angrier. He vowed to let that miserable inconsiderate asshole really have it when he got off at his floor. Finally, the elevator stopped and he turned in fury to face a blind elderly nun with a cane. He had taken the poking in his back personally and was going to give that insensitive bastard a real piece of his mind. Think about how wonderful your life would be if you took nothing personally. Think about how ineffective political ads would be if no one reacted to the negativity. I want to live in that place, as long as the weather's warm.

Now we venture into the future to answer more of the simple questions in life.

23. I WANT A PONY AND A MASERATI

A number of years ago, an extremely attractive couple entered my office. At first, they appeared to be the epitome of youthful exuberance and happiness. Both were teachers in their early thirties. He was straight out of GQ and she could easily have been a Vogue model. Obviously bright and well-spoken, they had a sad tale to tell about their communication skills. It appeared that they fought a great deal. Usually over trivial matters. These seemingly insignificant beginnings would then evolve into open warfare sometimes ending with her throwing the F bomb at him while he would try his best to avoid it. It had reached a point where they knew that someone would get hurt during one of their arguments. Hence counseling was deemed a good idea. First, the difficulties from her point of view.

"I have to say, right from the start, that I love him to pieces. We're a great couple and our problems appear to be getting worse as the years go by. We've been married for seven years now. For the most part, I'm very happy.

There are some things that he does that make me crazy and, by crazy, I mean frustrated and very angry. It's hard to explain this because it's not one thing. It's a lot of little things that add up until I explode.

For example, we went to a movie a few nights ago that was just horrible and almost impossible to sit through. He wanted to see it and I just went along for the ride. What a total waste of time.

About six months ago, we went on a vacation to the Caribbean to get away from it all. He picks an all inclusive hotel in Antigua where all the food at best was average. We really had no other meal options since everything was already included in the price. In addition, it seems that our hotel was a honeymoon destination so we were surrounded by twenty year olds constantly acting like children. Why would he pick a place like that for me?

Another example is the car we bought for me. He decided, after a few days of car shopping, that an Audi would be the right car for me. This car has more electronics than the moon shuttle and he knows how much difficulty I have with technology. Every time I get into the car I have to go through a five step process to play Spotify on my Bluetooth connection. Annoying to say the least and this is on an everyday basis. Once again, why would he pick something like that for me?

Then there's his choice of restaurants. It seems to me that almost every time we go out to eat, we have an argument over the restaurant. Let me be fair and say it's not every time but we argue much too much about where to eat. A few nights ago, we went to a restaurant known for their Peking duck. He thought it would be a great place to try and we'd never been there before. I told him that they should re-name the place rubber duck as I chewed mine for ten minutes just to be able to swallow the first bite. Also, we were seated near the kitchen and the noise was as ridiculous as everything we ate. Why would he take me to a place like that? He knows what I like and more importantly, what I don't like.

So you see, he's just totally out of tune with me and what I need. As I said, it's not one thing, it's a whole range of things that we fight about. Next week, we're going to look for a couch and a dining room set. I can guarantee right now that we will fight for two or three days until I explode out of total frustration. I would imagine that you'd like to hear this from his perspective so I yield to my partner in crime."

"Thank you sweetness. I'll try to be brief. Before I give you my perspective, I openly admit that I love her to pieces although I never really understood what that pieces thing really means. Since she has already given her perspective, it might be best if I explain my side of the story regarding the incidents she mentioned. Let's start with the choice of movies. If I were to wait for her to make a decision regarding what movie to see, it would take a week and the movie would be next seen on Netflix. In all the years that we have been together, I think she has chosen a movie no more than three or four times. She has a total inability to make decisions like this and then I am held responsible for the movie, the cold air conditioning or even the popcorn.

Regarding our vacation to Antigua, we had brochures from six different travel agencies and more than twenty-five hotels in our house for over two months. During that time, she would peruse them daily and could never come up with a decision regarding where to go. Finally, after two months of frustration, she said that she gave up and asked me to pick an island and a hotel to go to. She told me that it didn't make any difference to her anymore as they all looked very similar. So, I picked the island and the hotel. As usual, I became responsible for the food and everything on our trip. Why in God's name am I responsible for every aspect of a trip when she had the choices and the parameters for over two long months?

I finally figured out the rules to the game we play. Because she always defers to me and is unable to make decisions, she feels that she is able to criticize my choices. It took a great deal of time for me to figure this out. The main reason we're here, from my point of view, is to see if my theory is correct.

Let's talk about shopping for her car. What she didn't tell you was that we spent two full weekends looking for a car. On Saturday and Sunday of two successive weekends, we would start at nine o'clock in the morning and end at about five. Four full days of hell and fifteen visits to car dealerships. It was a hateful experience from beginning to end. As usual, she was unable to come to a decision. Finally, she asked me what I thought and I narrowed it down to three cars hoping that she would pick one. As the first car that I mentioned was the Audi, she told me that I was trying to tell her that she should get the Audi. No matter how many times I told her that it was her decision, she kept telling me that she knew that I wanted her to get the Audi. Ridiculous. Now, she wants to hold me responsible for anything that happens to the car. Probably even flat tires.

I could go on and on for hours and repeat basically the same story. As far as restaurants go, she has never- and I emphasize never- chosen a restaurant since we've been together. She'll tell me that she really doesn't care but when the meal is over, I feel as if I'm sitting with the food critic from the New York Times. She gives me credit for something that is impossible for me to do. She expects me to read her mind when it comes to decision making. I can't read her mind. Hell, at times I can't even read my own mind so how can I read hers. I think she refuses to take responsibility for choices so that she can be in a position to criticize.

Sometimes, I can even predict the future to some degree. As you know, we will be looking for a couch and a dining room set for our house. We will visit probably ten to twenty furniture stores during a two or three week period. She will make lists of all the stores visited and will note what dining room sets and sofas are possibilities. She will be unable or unwilling to make a decision and will try to defer to me. I will avoid indicating to her in any way what my choices would be because if I did I would be responsible for that furniture for the rest of my days.

After a few weeks, we will begin to argue and fight and she'll, somehow, twist the decision putting it into my hands despite all my efforts to avoid making a choice. This is a guarantee. This has happened every time we have to buy anything. I see no reason why the next shopping ventures wouldn't result in the same endings if nothing changes.

Why can't she just tell me what she wants?"

That was a really good question and I had some of the answers but not all. She had manipulated him over the years to be the fall guy regarding responsibility. She hated making decisions and refused to be held accountable. She was playing the blame game to the hilt and was winning because she was making all the rules. Aside from the psychodynamics involved, I suggested a practical approach to begin to put their discord back in line.

They told me that they had planned on going out to dinner on the upcoming Friday and Sunday nights. They also indicated that they expect to go to a movie on Saturday night. I advised him to sit back and have her make all the decisions regarding the restaurants and the movies. Under no condition was he to indicate, in any way, what his preferences would be. He totally agreed and she reluctantly agreed to the new master plan. The responsibility was to fall entirely on her and he was to take a decision making back seat. I knew it wouldn't work and it didn't.

The next week when they came for their session, I found out that they didn't go to a movie or eat out. It appears that she was so angry at having to make three decisions that she had a total meltdown and refused to talk to him for two days. I'm happy to report that we all worked together for a number of months and the major issues were resolved. For a while, she was less than enamored with me but that's the price you pay when you get paid for being honest.

Many people find it extremely hard to say what they want.

For some, it is a feeling of selfishness that stops them in their tracks. For others, it could be a case of a little too much consideration for the needs and wants of others. Children have no difficulty whatsoever with telling us what they want. When my son was four I asked him what he wanted for his upcoming fifth birthday and he told me that he wanted a pony. My daughter, when asked at the tender age of twelve, told me she wanted a red Ferrari. We seem to lose the ability to say what we want and become more and more reliant on other people's ability to read our minds.

A number of years ago, with another birthday looming on the horizon I was asked by a friend what my plans were. I told him that I usually wait to see what other people suggest and go along with their plans. He told me that he always plans his own birthday and invites whomever he wants to do something that he really wants to do. Sounded a bit egotistical at the time but I decided to try it for my own birthday. I picked a lunch at a restaurant on the beach with sixteen friends. We ate, we drank and I had a ball. It was a wonderful idea. Nowadays, if someone should ask what I would like to do for any occasion, I have no difficulty telling them what I want. Why should I leave it to chance and hope that they guess instead of simply voicing my preferences.

So, the question should be asked of you. What do you want? You should define your wants operationally. What I mean by this is the fact that you have to be specific and the want needs to be achievable. For example, if you say that your goal is to be happy, you've picked an undefinable goal. You need to figure out what the specific things are that will make you happy and the range of items could run into the thousands. For the same reason, you can't say that you want to be rich or that you want to be a Broadway star. You need to define the steps along the way so that it makes sense to you.

Nowadays, many young people say that they want to be entrepreneurs. When you ask them what that means they, oftentimes, tell you that they want to work for themselves and they want to make a substantial amount of money. If you define this operationally, a plan is needed to get from point A to point B.It has to makes sense and be realistic. The plan may include saving money to invest in a business, going back to school, working for a particular firm to get experience and a plethora of other steps.

This question of what you want needs to be asked and answered in a number of different areas. You can pose this question with regards to your lifestyle, relationships, birthdays, jobs, travel, sex life, retirement and many, many other areas of daily living. Plan the steps to get what you want once you are able to honestly answer the initial question. After all, how can you tell where you are in life if you never made a decision as to where you planned to be?

24. OKAY CAPTAIN, SET A COURSE

What now? Where does this all lead me? Two good questions now that you are aware of the fact that there are no magical solutions to the multiple difficulties that we all encounter in life. Before we tackle these two questions, I want you to bear with me and read the following eleven everyday sayings that we've heard throughout our lives.

- Today is the first day of the rest of your life.
- No matter where you go, there you are.
- It's not the years in your life that count. It's the life in your years.
- Life is what happens when you're busy making other plans.
- All good things must come to an end.
- I have learned that you can't please everyone, so don't try.
- Be happy with who you are and not who people think you are.

- Extra crispy KFC can serve as a diet food (this one I claim as mine).
- Life is not a fairy tale. If you lose a slipper at midnight, you're drunk.
- Never take life too seriously, no one gets out alive.
- Hearses do not have luggage racks.

Of course, you've heard these maxims through the years. As you read the list, you were probably rolling your eyes by the time you reached the bottom. Since we all know these trite little sayings, why can't we just do what they say. The good news is that with the exception of the chicken saying, all the proverbs are absolutely true. Another saying that I like was not included on my list and refers to everyone being the captain of their own ship. As a captain, your responsibility is to set a course and then make mid-course corrections as you go on your way. To help you chart your journey, I have summarized the book in an abbreviated form and separated the book into five major areas. The following five areas should be kept in mind if you want to avoid floundering on submerged rocks.

1. Live in the real world and think as logically as you possibly can. Remember that this is not a rehearsal and do-overs only count in stickball.
2. Have short-term, mid-term and long-term plans and goals. Identify your mistakes and vow to stop repeating them in the future as you

move closer to happiness and contentment.
Yes, happiness and contentment.

3. Strive to know yourself. Including the good, the bad and the ugly. Take stock and look at yourself emotionally, physically, intellectually and spiritually. Make attempts to self-advocate and be more selfish (in the good sense) as you move forward.

4. Embrace the idea of determining when enough is enough. Strive for good balance in your life between the past, present and future. Remember that, as you move ahead through murky waters, everything is relative and that timing is everything.

5. Never be afraid. This is actually the crux of everything. If you plan and allow yourself options the surprises that pop up in life will not throw you completely off your planned course. There are definitely sudden changes that are out of our control that may alter our lives such as illness and the like. Should this happen, it will require taking out a new chart and planning accordingly within the framework of reality.

There I've said it all and I'm glad. It's time to either start your engines or get your oars ready. You determine the speed and you determine the course. Have a wonderful trip and never, never be afraid.

CHAPTER 25

The beginning.